AIRFIX
magazine guide 14

American Fighters of World War 2

Alan W Hall

Patrick Stephens Ltd
in association with Airfix Products Ltd

No part of this publication may be
reproduced, stored in a retrieval
system or transmitted, in any form or
by any means, electronic, mechanical,
photocopying, recording or
otherwise, without prior permission
in writing from Patrick Stephens Ltd

First published — 1976

ISBN 0 85059 225 9

Cover design by Tim McPhee

Text set in 8 on 9 pt Helvetica Medium
by Blackfriars Press Limited,
Leicester.
Printed on Fineblade cartridge 90 gsm
and bound by the Garden City Press,
Letchworth, Herts.
Published by Patrick Stephens
Limited, Bar Hill, Cambridge, CB3 8EL,
in association with Airfix Products
Limited, London SW18

Contents

Editor's introduction

IN this, the second book Alan Hall has written on the fighter aircraft used in World War 2, the same theme has been followed. He has attempted to show the development of both US Army Air Force and US Navy aircraft in two separate sections, for apart from some necessary co-operation the two sides acted almost independently during the conflict.

The book has been written simply, with a younger audience in mind, but I hope that the facts given will provide even the more sophisticated reader with something of value for the reference library.

It has been difficult to keep the number of words to within the limits of these pages as so much can be written about such famous aircraft as the Corsair, Mustang and Thunderbolt. The author has, however, added a number of other aircraft types such as the Bearcat and Tigercat in US Navy service that are essential to the overall picture of fighter aircraft of World War 2 as they were conceived and built in prototype form between 1941 and 1945. They also serve as a link between the old Army Air Corps days and the present day USAF which was created two years after the war ended. The US Navy, on the other hand, has not changed its air associations since the Bureau of Aeronautics was set up in 1920, although more recently, aircraft designations have at last been standardised for both services.

Nowhere in the brief history of aviation have there been such large numbers of aircraft available to any nation than there were in use by the United States in World War 2. The mere contemplation of such power has, I hope, been reflected in this description of the aircraft in use at that time.

BRUCE QUARRIE

America in isolation

Appalled by the wanton waste of human life and material in World War 1, the United States adopted a political attitude of isolation from Europe and as a result was totally unprepared for the outbreak of the second conflict 25 years later. This attitude, coupled with the financial crisis of the mid-1930s, reflected itself in numerous ways, one of which was the development of many unrealistic attitudes to air power.

Any student of the United States armed forces knows that the rivalry between the Army and Navy reached almost stupid proportions between the wars and even during the 1941 to '45 period was still prevalent. The products of the Army Academy and its Naval equivalent would have nothing to do with each other, and policies about aircraft procurement, combined operations, even designations of aircraft, were completely separated.

By putting both of these considerations together it is possible to understand why the Americans were unable to hold the Japanese advance across the Pacific, were totally unprepared for the Pearl Harbour attack, and took some time to recover before eventually taking the initiative and regaining control of the situation on land, sea and in the air.

Luckily, the American nation has vast resources of manpower and this, combined with an alert and powerful industry, was able to regain the many losses incurred immediately after the United States entered the war.

All considerations of US policy must be made in two classifications, the Navy and Army, and in the two main theatres of war, the European and Pacific. For example, at this distance in time it is not readily remembered that until 1943 the Americans were using almost entirely obsolete aircraft such as the P-40 Warhawk by the Army and early versions of the Wildcat and even the Brewster F2A in the Navy. It was not until 1943 that the 8th Air Force in England got the B-24 and B-17 in quantity and much later before they could be adequately escorted by P-47 Thunderbolts and P-51 Mustangs. In fact, the policy of daylight bombing almost came to a grinding halt due to the heavy losses sustained by the bombers still working on the pre-war theory that heavily armed bomber aircraft were bound to break through enemy fighter defences.

The American Navy had much to be thankful for in the Grumman designs started immediately before the war and developed through the F4F Wildcat, F6F Hellcat and F8F Bearcat. The following histories of these aircraft fully illustrate the way in which this aircraft manufacturer was able to rush through the prototype and development stages of fighter aircraft to such an extent that in some cases squadrons were receiving aircraft within 18 months of the first prototype having flown.

Similarly, the Army Air Force was helped considerably by American industry in sorting itself out and getting the right sort of aircraft with which to fight the battle. The prime example here is the development of the P-51 Mustang. If it had not been for the intervention of General 'Hap' Arnold, the most famous fighter of all time might not have reached squadron status and even so, many of the advantages gained came from British ideas of producing a Merlin-engined variant.

It is estimated that the US aircraft industry produced no less than 101,500 fighters of nine main types during the four years that America was at war. Not only did they supply their own forces with ever-increasing numbers, but also became the free world's arsenal in implementing the greatest aid that could ever have been given to their Allies by the Lease-Lend agreements signed in March 1941. The Soviet Union had much of its outdated air force re-equipped rapidly by vast supplies of fighters and bombers from the United States at a time when Russia was reeling under the hammer blows of the German blitzkrieg. Similarly, Britain, with only so much war manufacturing potential, leaned heavily on American supplies of aircraft for both the Fleet Air Arm and the RAF. The other nations of the world such as the French and many of the Commonwealth countries bordering the Pacific could not have had sufficient supplies of aircraft in any way unless they had been supplied from Lease-Lend funds.

American airpower, like the other parts of the armed forces, was reduced to almost nothing after the great demobilisation at the end of World War 1. After all, it was said this was the 'war to end all wars' and there was no need for any further armaments. The air force survived with obsolete aircraft to such an extent that there was little to re-organise when it was decided in 1920 that the US Army should set up a separate air service within its ranks. Leading personalities such as General 'Billy' Mitchell campaigned vigorously for up-to-date aircraft and in his case favoured the view that the bomber aircraft was supreme. He proved it by organising a bombing attack on some US Navy warships which, due to direct hits, were badly damaged or sunk. This had never been proved before but one vital thing was forgotten and that was the opposition from the enemy on the ground and his fighter forces in defence.

The Army Air Corps did eventually receive more modern equipment, but emphasis was laid on bombers, such as the gigantic XB-19 and the early version of the B-17 Flying Fortress, that little thought was left for fighters.

On the US Navy side a Bureau of Aeronautics was set up in 1920 to administer the procurement and advise on the use of aircraft in warfare at sea. The first US aircraft carrier, the Langley, was converted from a collier called the Jupiter in 1922, and several battleships were given catapults and light observation aircraft to go with them. The first real carriers that the US Navy acquired were the Saratoga and Lexington which, at the time, were the largest of their kind in the world. On the aircraft side, however, the Navy was not so bright. It persisted in the idea that the biplane fighter was supreme, but by the late thirties these types had been superseded by monoplane fighters with enclosed cockpits and retractable undercarriages.

By 1944, in the space of two years, the US Navy had built up its air arm to have 16,500 aircraft and 30 aircraft carriers in service. There had even been some limited co-operation between Navy and Army units when Lt Col Doolittle led the famous raid on the Japanese mainland with 16 B-25 Mitchell bombers from the deck of the carrier Hornet. Similarly, the Navy recognised that as a matter of necessity it had to give in to the Army's demand to use its long range patrol aircraft for operations over the Atlantic and in co-operation with carrier fleets.

On the other hand, if it had not been for naval actions the Army would not have been able to take its giant B-29 bombers to islands like Saipan, Guam, and Iwo Jima, from which attacks were launched on Japan itself, ending with the dropping of the atomic bombs on Hiroshima and Nagasaki.

On September 18 1947 the US Army dropped all connections with its air element and the United States Air Force came into being in its own right. Since then the US Army has built up another air force of its own but this time for direct co-operation with troop movements and for battlefield reconnaissance, using, in the main, helicopters.

America's isolationist policy that led to its unpreparedness in 1941 is also a thing of the past. In its place two 'minor' wars in Korea and Viet Nam, both of which cost the US dearly in men and material, have shown the need for international co-operation to prevent war.

US Army Air Force aircraft

Bell P-39 Airacobra

The Bell P-39 was probably one of the most controversial fighters that saw service during World War 2. It was used initially by the Army Air Corps, and was bought by the British Purchasing Commission for RAF use by a contract issued on April 13 1940.

The Airacobra could be described as a large cannon with an aircraft built round it. Bell designers, led by Bob Wood, were intrigued by the American Armament Corporation (AAC) 37 mm T-9 gun which had been demonstrated in May 1935 and its potential not properly realised.

Early in the design stage it was decided to locate the cannon on the aircraft centre line for optimum effect, which therefore dictated that the engine position should be behind the cockpit. This also involved the use of a tricycle undercarriage, making the XP-39 prototype unconventional to say the least.

The Air Corps signed a contract on October 7 1937 for a single prototype and the first machine (38-326) was flown at Dayton, Ohio, in April 1938 by James Taylor, the Company Test Pilot. Initial tests were satisfactory and the Army ordered a service test batch of 12 YP-39s and one YP-39A which had no turbo-supercharger.

During the early trials NACA gave the XP-39 a close examination and recommended a number of rather major design changes. These included altering the radiators to a wing root type, with leading edge intakes, lowering the cockpit canopy, placing a carburettor air scoop under the fuselage, and the deletion of the turbo-supercharger. Bell made the changes required and the prototype was redesignated XP-39B. An immediate improvement in performance was obtained and on August 10 1939 the fighter was ordered into full production, with the Army requiring 80 examples immediately. The first 20 aircraft were delivered from January 1941 onwards and were P-39Cs which had leak-proof fuel tanks and four .30 inch wing guns replacing the two of similar calibre in the nose. Provision was also made for a 500 lb bomb or a 75 gallon drop tank to be placed under the centre fuselage.

The first order for the P-39D variant was placed in September 1940 for 369 aircraft but 60 of the earlier contract were modified to 'D' model standard. Deliveries began in April 1941 and at about the same time the first export

'The cannon with the fighter built round it' . . . *an adequate description of the unconventional Airacobra. This version is a P-39N having a 20 mm nose cannon and six .30 inch machine-guns in the wings and cowling.*

version of the Airacobra appeared.

The British Purchasing Commission had ordered 179 Airacobras which were initially called Caribous but later had their name changed to conform with the US original.

The plan was to buy 675 of these aircraft but in fact only one squadron ever became operational with the RAF as the machine did not come up to the expectations of the British and it was eventually scrapped.

Over 250 British Airacobras were made available for the Soviet Air Force as part of British aid to Russia and nearly 200 were re-acquired by the USAAF in Britain at the end of 1942. A further 200 had also been repossessed by the USAAF in December 1941 after the Japanese attack at Pearl Harbour.

Returning to the P-39D, this first saw service when it replaced the earlier 'C' model with the 31st Pursuit Group at Selfridge Field, Michigan, in April 1941. When the Japanese attacked, the few aircraft then available were deployed along the west coast of the United States in anticipation of Japanese bombing raids.

As more Airacobras became avail-

This Airacobra is probably a P-39D judging by the national insignia and the date of the picture. It differed little from the later versions and was the first of the type to see action with the 347th Fighter Group at Guadalcanal.

able they were moved to forward bases in Alaska and the Panama Canal Zone, whilst in March 1942 the 8th Pursuit Group became the first P-39 unit to be deployed in Australia.

This came at an opportune time as the Japanese were raiding Darwin in Australia and the Airacobras of the 8th were deployed to Port Moresby to gain combat experience. It was here that the first two pilots flying Airacobras shot down enemy aircraft during a mission on April 6.

By the 30th of that month 26 P-39Ds of the 35th and 26th Squadrons of the 8th Pursuit Group had claimed 40 enemy aircraft destroyed but had lost almost as many aircraft in combat and accidents as their opponents.

The next unit to join the fight against the Japanese was the 35th fighter group which relieved the 8th at Port Moresby. The aircraft were, how-

American Fighters of World War 2

Bell P-39Q-21, one of the main export versions of the aircraft. It has the unusual modification of a four-bladed propeller and under fuselage long range fuel tank. Russian markings have been applied.

ever, frequently out-manoeuvred by the Japanese Zeros but the gallantry of the pilots involved impressed even their adversaries.

Elsewhere the Airacobra saw service with the 34th Fighter Group which operated against the Japanese in Alaska and the Aleutian Islands, between May 1942 and January 1943. The 32nd, 36th and 53rd Fighter Groups operated in the Panama Canal Zone with the Airacobra for many months but in the Continental United States the aircraft was used only by replacement training units and for forming and training fighter groups before being sent overseas with more modern aircraft.

The USAAF's Pacific operations with the P-39 were not particularly impressive but at least they represented a useful contribution to the delaying action made necessary by the rapid Japanese advances, and during the critical months of 1942 supplemented the available air power until more modern fighters could be produced. On the other hand Airacobra operations in Europe proved to be a costly failure.

For a short time, immediately after America's entry into the war, the 342nd Composite Group took their P-39s to Iceland but it was the 31st Fighter Group from Selfridge Field — the first unit to be equipped with the aircraft — that had the task of flying the aircraft operationally against the Luftwaffe.

Only one mission, in July 1942, was flown from British bases during which six out of 12 aircraft were lost without damage to the enemy. As a result the Group very hurriedly changed to flying Spitfire Vbs.

It had already been recognised that the Airacobra, due to the deletion of the turbo supercharger on the engine, was of little value at high or medium altitudes as an interceptor. It became relegated to fighter-bomber duties and in this role went to North Africa with the 81st and 350th Fighter Groups and was also used by two squadrons of the 68th Reconnaissance Group. Providing adequate fighter cover could be given, the P-39 was very successfully operated in this low-level role. One more unit, the 332nd Fighter Group, converted to the type in this theatre, and although eventually replaced by Thunderbolts and Lightnings, did yeoman service against both troop and armour concentrations. All Airacobras were phased out of active service by late 1944.

In spite of the difficulties encountered with the operational use of the aircraft, development and production of the P-39 continued at high pressure, not only to meet Army requirements but also for overseas Lease-Lend supply. Out of a total of 9,558 aircraft built, the Russians received no less than 4,773. Deliveries started in 1942 with 336 P-39Ds which had the 37 mm cannon deleted and replaced by one of 20 mm calibre, like the British version.

The P-39F followed which had an Aeroproducts propeller replacing the Curtiss type and 229 were built.

Changes in the G, K and L variants differed only in engine types and propellers used. A larger diameter propeller, for example, was used on the P-39M, of which 240 were built.

The final production versions were, in fact, the most numerous to be produced and the P-39N and P-39Q were the principal Lease-Lend variants sent to Russia. Production totalled 2,095. Final batches had a four-bladed propeller which gave better performance at low-level and modifications in the underwing armament were also made.

Bell P-39 Airacobra Specification
Type Single-seat fighter-bomber.
Power plant One, 1,150 hp Allison V-1710-35 12-cylinder liquid-cooled engine.
Performance Max speed 335 mph at 10,000 feet. Range 600 miles (clean). Ceiling 32,100 feet.
Dimensions Span 34 feet. Length 30 feet 2 inches. Height 11 feet 10 inches.
Armament One 37 mm or 20 mm cannon firing through the airscrew hub. Four .50 inch machine-guns in wings. Provision for 500 lb bomb or long range fuel tank.

Bell P-63 Kingcobra

Following the disastrous entry into service of the Airacobra, in the European theatre of operations, the USAAC soon realised that its unconventional design was of little use as an interceptor. During the development phase of the aircraft three XP-39Es were built during 1941 using D model fuselages but having laminar-flow wings, angular tail units and Allison V-1710-47 engines.

These prototypes differed so considerably from the original Airacobra that they were given the designation XP-63 and the first flew on December 7 1942 followed by the second on Feb-

Above *High above the clouds this Bell-63A-6 Kingcobra was one which eventually was exported to the Russians. It was equipped with a 37 mm cannon firing through the propeller hub and two .50 inch machine-guns in blisters under the wings.* **Below** *P-63C Kingcobra of which 1,227 were built. Compare this view with that of the Airacobra noting the differing laminar wing shape and the equitapered fin and rudder.*

American Fighters of World War 2

ruary 5 1943.

Both prototypes were lost at an early stage in their trials due to accidents but a third aircraft, designated XP-63A, took to the air on April 26 1943. This variant had provision for external bombs and was powered by a similar Allison engine but of increased horsepower. A further proposal to fit a Packard Merlin into this aircraft was abandoned.

Meanwhile, Lease-Lend deliveries to the Russians of Airacobras had been most successful. The Soviet Air Force found the machine to be ideally suited to their requirements. The proposal of an improved version was therefore immediately accepted and the P-63 went into production for export.

Bell built 1,725 of this model and deliveries began late in 1942.

The basic armament again comprised one 37 mm cannon in the nose and a .50 inch machine-gun in each wing. Provision was made for either a 522 lb bomb, a 75 or a 175 gallon fuel tank under the centre section and two wing racks were later added for other 525 lb bombs or additional fuel tanks. The Russians also added stations for three rocket projectiles under each wing.

In addition to the Russians, the French Air Force received 300 P-63Cs. These differed in having an uprated engine and a ventral fin under the tail unit.

Several other variants were produced including one which had a clear bubble canopy, and the P-63E was given a ten inch greater wing span in May 1945 but only 13 were built before the war's end and contracts for a further 2,930 were cancelled. Two P-63Fs were also tested in 1945 and these, although similar to the E model, had a taller fin and rudder with a small dorsal extension.

The USAAF used a special version of the P-63 in 1943 as a manned target aircraft which could actually be shot at by trainee fighter pilots. Based on the P-63A-9, the first five examples were designated RP-63A-11s and had all armament and armour removed. The entire fuselage and wings had reinforced and toughened external skins and the canopy was largely covered in. Frangible bullets were used by the attacking aircraft and a red light blinked on the wing tips when hits were registered. The name 'Pinball' was unofficially given to the RP-63 because of the similarity to the machines used in gaming parlours throughout the United States.

An initial 95 aircraft were built followed by another 200 designated RP-63Cs. The RP-63G had a Allison V-1710-135 engine and 32 were built. The designation of these targets was later changed to QF-63, but although this prefix indicated a pilotless target drone none were used in this capacity.

The Kingcobra was a fast aircraft having a top speed of 408 mph at 24,450 feet. Several still survive and at least one is used today in high performance air races in the United States.

Bell P-63 Kingcobra Specification

Type Single-seat fighter, fighter-bomber and target aircraft.

Power plant One 1,325 hp Allison V-1710-93 12-cylinder liquid-cooled engine.

Performance Max speed 361 mph at 5,000 feet. Max cruising speed 378 mph. Range 390 miles. Ceiling 43,000 feet.

Dimensions Span 38 feet 4 inches. Length 32 feet 8 inches. Height 12 feet 7 inches.

Armament One 37 mm cannon and two .50 inch machine-guns. Provision for one to three 522 lb bombs.

Bell P-59 Airacomet

The United States aircraft industry, due mainly to the fact that it was slow in gearing up for war production, did not have the expertise of its British and German rivals in aero engine development. This became evident as no work had been done on gas turbine power plants on which both Germany and Britain had been working since before the war.

Once America had entered the war all British development secrets were made available to the USAAF who in

turn requested the Bell Aircraft Corporation to undertake the development of a jet fighter design in September 1941.

Work proceeded in great secrecy and as rapidly as development of the new engine allowed. To add to the confidential nature of the work the USAAF designated the project XP-59A which was the same as a new radial-engine twin-boom pusher fighter design being developed by Bell at the same time. The latter design was eventually stopped and the P-59 took the designation in its own right.

Construction of the first airframe began in the spring of 1942 and was a simple, conventional mid-wing monoplane design. It had a slender fuselage, conventional construction and the two jet engines were carried on each side of the fuselage under the wings. A tricycle undercarriage was employed with the main legs retracting into the wings.

Three XP-59As and a service trials batch of 13 YP-59As were ordered, the first of which was completed in late 1942 when the prototype was moved to Muroc (later Edwards Air Force base) for flight testing.

Meanwhile, the development of General Electric Type I-A turbo-jets had been going ahead steadily, based on Whittle-type originals. Several of the latter had previously been sent to the United States and a Gloster Meteor was sent to Edwards for flight evaluation.

The first engine was bench-tested on March 18 1942 and was expected to develop 1,400 lb st.

With both of the prototype engines installed the XP-59A started taxi tests

The serial on this wartime picture of the P-59 Airacomet has been censored but it is probably one of the aircraft used by the experimental 412th Fighter Group which was specially formed to carry out trials with the aircraft.

on September 30 1942 and was flown for the first time by Robert M. Stanley, Bell's Chief Test Pilot, on October 1.

Initial tests proved that the revolutionary new aircraft had a top speed of 404 mph at 25,000 feet. This was somewhat below expectations and problems were encountered with the engine installation as it was found to give an inordinate amount of aerodynamic interference and the aircraft was subject to 'snaking' in level flight.

The first pre-production models of the Airacomet which had been ordered in March 1942 were subsequently fitted with an improved version of the General Electric engine which gave 1,650 lb st and the first flight was made in August 1943. Little improvement in performance over the prototypes was noted and it was therefore decided that the Airacomet would be ordered primarily for use as a trainer until later single-seaters were available using improvements in jet power which were then being developed.

The first 20 production machines were designated P-59A, and although similar to the prototype were slightly longer and had a shorter fin and rudder. The engines were again uprated to 2,000 lb st and given the type designation J31-GE-3s.

A production order for 100 P-59As was placed shortly before the prototype's initial flight, but in view of the

American Fighters of World War 2

One of the French P-36s delivered before the start of the war in all silver finish. These aircraft fought with distinction although not all of the total order had been delivered by the time of the capitulation.

disappointing performance of the fighter this production order was halved on October 30 1943 by which time the Airacomet was no longer considered to be more than an experimental aircraft. Bell designers, by that time, had already started on another jet powered aircraft, the XP-80, but as the company already had extensive commitments in other directions the project was turned over to Lockheed and the P-80 became the first operational fighter for the USAF.

All P-59s were issued to the 412th Fighter Group, an especially formed trials unit in the 4th Air Force for operational evaluation. They were also used for a wide variety of test work and some were eventually modified as drone directors with an open front cockpit ahead of the pilot. This modification was made on the original prototype XP-59A which first flew with an observer on October 30 1942.

Although the Airacomet was not a success as a fighter it had a powerful armament in the nose. This consisted of one 37 mm and three .50 inch forward-firing guns, but the type proved to be a poor gun platform because of the engine instability and was therefore not proceeded with.

The Airacomet was, however, a significant aircraft in the development of United States air power and as such is an important machine despite its limited use.

Bell P-59 Airacomet Specification

Type   Single-seat fighter and training aircraft.

Power plant   Two 2,000 lb st General Electric J31-GE-5 turbojets.

Performance   Maximum speed 413 mph at 30,000 feet. Max cruising speed 375 mph at 30,000 feet. Ceiling 46,200 feet.

Dimensions   Span 45 feet 6 inches. Length 38 feet 10 inches. Height 12 feet 4 inches.

Armament   One 37 mm cannon and three .50 inch machine-guns in the nose plus two 1,000 lb bombs or eight 60 lb rockets.

Curtiss P-36 Hawk

The Curtiss P-36 was perhaps the first of a long line of successful American fighter designs which started in the mid-1930s and brought forth a generation of high performance monoplanes in time for World War 2 combat. Prior to the introduction of the P-36, the Army Air Corps had produced large numbers of biplane fighters which, although extremely manoeuvrable, were totally outclassed by European designs then progressing from prototype to production status.

The Curtiss P-36 and Seversky P-35 were the subjects of a design competition held by the Army Air Corps in 1935 and 1936 to secure the first single-seat Pursuit monoplane to have retractable undercarriage and enclosed cockpit.

The Curtiss company, with a long line of Hawk biplanes already produced for the Air Corps, began work on its own privately financed prototype, the Curtiss 75, in November 1934. It was submitted to Wright Field for the design competition in May 1935 and at that time was the only entry. The machine was powered by a 900 hp Wright R-1670 two-row radial engine and was of all-metal construction. One of the novel features was the fact that the main legs of the undercarriage rotated through 90 degrees and retracted into the wings. The armament comprised two .30 inch machine-guns on the cowling firing through the airscrew arc.

Two subsequent design competitions, at which other aircraft such as the P-35 were included, led eventually to three service test models of the Hawk 75 being ordered in July 1936. The Seversky machine also won a production order.

The first three machines, known as YP-36s, were delivered in February 1937 and were powered by 1,050 hp Pratt & Whitney R-1830-13 engines. The cockpit was modified from the private venture aircraft to improve the forward and rear views, and a retractable tail wheel was also included. USAAC tests on these three aircraft produced a contract on July 7 1937 for 210 examples valued at about $4,000,000. It became the largest peace-time contract that the Air Corps had ever awarded for fighter aircraft production.

Deliveries to fighter squadrons began in April 1938, the first 178 aircraft being P-36As, and the production run was concluded in the first month of 1939 with 31 P-36Cs. These had an additional .30 inch machine-gun in each wing and an uprated engine.

The early examples had various teething troubles which were overcome by February 1941 and the P-36 was sent overseas for the first time. The 23rd Pursuit Squadron moved to Elmendorf, Alaska, and at the same time the 46th and 47th Pursuit Squadrons moved their bases to Hawaii. It was these aircraft flying from Wheeler Field that intercepted the first Japanese bombers taking part in the attack on Pearl Harbour on December 7 1941. Four P-36As of the 46th Pursuit Squadron intercepted enemy aircraft in the second phase of the attack and destroyed two of them.

Perhaps the principal feature of these Hawk 75s was the fact that Curtiss exported as many as they produced for the USAAC. The main customer was France and here 100 aircraft were ordered, differing slightly from the standard P-36 in having Browning machine-guns, reverse throttle operation and metric calibrated instruments. The first aircraft of the batch reached Le Havre on December 24 1938 and went into service in March 1939 with the 4e and 5e *Escadre de Chasse* based at Reims. The French Air Force won its first victories over the Western Front using Hawk 75 fighters. On December 8 1939 five of the American fighters destroyed two Bf 109Es in a brief engagement.

The complete order had not been delivered by the time the French capitulated in 1940. In fact, an additional 135 machines had been requested but most of these did not arrive. Several were disembarked at French colonial ports and were used in Morocco and the Lebanon. Many of the machines fell into German hands, some still in their delivery crates, and these were transported to Germany where they were assembled and sold to Finland for use against the Russians in the war between the two countries.

Another Government ordering the Hawk 75 was Norway. A total of 30 Hawk 75A-8s were on order when Norway fell. The machines were subsequently sent to Canada as advanced trainers and used by Norwegian forces there. Later, these machines were presented to the Peruvian Air Force.

All outstanding contracts on the French order were hurriedly transferred to Britain after the fall of France. The RAF received 227 Hawk 75A fighters, originally intended for France, and the type was promptly given the name Mohawk. The machines were fitted with six .30 inch machine-guns and British equipment, but did not see active service, being held in reserve at various RAF maintenance units until the end of 1941 when they were shipped to India for use by

A pre-war picture of two P-36s of the 191st Fighter Squadron. Squadron insignia on the fuselage sides replaced national markings.

the Indian Air Force. Those that went to the Far East remained operational on the Burma Front until finally replaced in December 1943.

The South African Air Force also operated the Mohawk in the Middle East. No 3 Squadron used these machines on limited operations and in the autumn of 1941 others were supplied to the Portuguese Air Force. The Iranian Government had ordered ten Cyclone-powered Hawk 75A-9 fighters which reached that country shortly before it was occupied by British and Russian Forces in August 1941. The machines were still in their original shipping crates and were transferred to the maintenance unit at Karachi and subsequently issued to No 5 Squadron RAF which operated them on the Burma Front.

The only other export order for the Hawk 75 was that placed by the Netherlands Government who expected delivery of 35 machines.

These were later reduced to 24 and, as they could not be delivered to the Netherlands after the German invasion, they were diverted to the East Indies where they arrived in 1940 entering service with the Dutch Army Air Corps and taking part in the resistance to the Japanese invasion.

The Curtiss P-36/Hawk 75 saw service in more foreign Air Forces than it did in the USAAC. It did, however, serve as the basis for a long line of Curtiss fighters, all of which subsequently forsook the radial engine for in-line versions. It was doubtless the forerunner of many of the more successful American designs.

Curtiss P-36 Specification

Type Single-seat interceptor fighter.
Power plant One 1,200 hp Pratt & Whitney R-1830-17 Twin Wasp radial air-cooled engine.
Performance Max speed 311 mph at 10,000 feet. Max cruising speed 270 mph.

Range 820 miles.
Dimensions Span 37 feet 4 inches. Length 28 feet 6 inches. Height 9 feet 6 inches.
Armament Three .30 inch machine-guns and provision for underwing stores.

Curtiss P-40A Tomahawk

The Curtiss P-40 was a direct descendant of the Hawk 75 (P-36) as its design was basically the same with the exception that it used an in-line engine. During its service career the P-40 had many shortcomings, notably its poor altitude performance, but at that time the Americans had no suitable engine with which to produce a high altitude performance aircraft.

The aim of the earlier experiments with the XP-40, ordered in July 1937, was to increase the flying qualities of the P-36. In fact the prototype was the tenth production P-36A reworked to incorporate an Allison V-1710-19 liquid-cooled engine which it was thought would produce a better performance than the existing air-cooled radials of comparable power.

The machine was flown for the first time in October 1938 and the USAAC awarded it what at that time was the largest ever production order for an American fighter. A contract was signed on April 27 1939 for the delivery of 524 machines.

The prototype underwent many modifications during its early trials. The most important external difference was the removal of the engine coolant radiator from beneath the rear fuselage and its repositioning in the nose under the propeller. Armament on this first version comprised one .30 inch and one .50 inch machine-gun in the nose. It had a top speed of 342 mph at 12,200 feet.

By the time that production P-40s appeared in May 1940, several other changes had been made from the original prototype. Firstly, an Allison V-1710-33 engine rated at 1,040 hp at 15,000 feet was installed, and intakes for a single stage supercharger were introduced above the nose.

No pre-production prototypes were produced and the first three P-40s off the line went for service trials. A further 197 were delivered to the USAAF by September 1940 but the remaining 324 of the original contract were not proceeded with due to the urgency of the French requirement for Hawk 81A-1 fighters at that time.

As it happened, none of these were delivered until after the French collapse and the order was taken over by the RAF. Still bearing French instrumentation and cockpit layout, these machines were designated Tomahawk Mks I, IA and IB.

The immediate British need was for sufficient aircraft to stem a possible

Curtiss Mohawk IV in RAF service. Most of these aircraft were former French air force machines which were diverted after the French collapse.

American Fighters of World War 2

Two post-war pictures of Curtiss P-40s still in existence. Both these machines have been repainted to represent either an RAF or a USAAC aircraft and appear at various air days in the United States (Aviation Photo News).

German invasion in 1940. This threat, however, receded, though further Tomahawk deliveries were made. These were IIAs, most of which went to the Middle East via West Africa. Other urgent orders were received from the Chinese who had 100 to bolster their own fighter defence; 49 were shipped direct to the Soviet Union and others were supplied to the Turkish Air Force in 1942.

Very few P-40 Tomahawks reached the USAAC and although 62 were based at Hawaii, the majority of these were destroyed on the ground by the Japanese surprise attack on December 7.

It should be emphasised that the USAAC never used the name Tomahawk for their early P-40s. Later versions of the basic design did indeed receive a name, Warhawk, but this was not until later. The development of this aircraft will be seen in the next section.

Curtiss P-40 Tomahawk Specification
Type Single-seat interceptor fighter.
Power plant One 1,200 hp Allison V-1710-33 12-cylinder in-line liquid-cooled engine.
Performance Max speed 352 mph at 15,000 feet. Max cruising speed 278 mph. Range 945 miles. Ceiling 32,400 feet.

Dimensions Span 37 feet 3½ inches. Length 31 feet 8 inches. Height 10 feet 7 inches.

Armament Two .50 inch and two or four .30 inch machine-guns.

Curtiss P-40D and P-40M Warhawk

Early in 1940 the Curtiss designers, realising that both the P-36 and P-40, at that time in service, were inadequate against either German or Japanese fighters, sought to redesign the basic Hawk 81A to take an improved power plant and consequently have better performance.

The same basic fuselage and wing shapes were employed but armour and self-sealing fuel tanks were added and the armament was greatly increased to six .50 inch machine-guns in the light of lessons learned in the Battle of Britain. At the same time an under-fuselage rack was incorporated for a 500 lb bomb or a long range fuel tank. Armour was incorporated and the whole design reworked around the best available Allison engine.

Now known as the Hawk 87-1, the first orders for the modified fighter came from a British contract of May 1940. The order called for 560 aircraft which the RAF named Kittyhawk I. The machine flew for the first time on May 22 1941, by which time the USAAF had placed an order for the same aircraft, designated P-40D. A large percentage of the British order, which was by then under Lease-Lend rules, was sent to the Royal Australian Air Force. Even the RAF's own machines were sent overseas and served with distinction in the Western Desert where, from June 1942 onwards, aircraft of this type caused great havoc amongst Rommel's armour.

In 1941 a further development, which followed closely on the same lines as that of the P-51 Mustang, involved the installation of a Rolls-Royce Merlin 28 in a P-40D airframe. This became known as the XP-40F and first flew on June 30 1941. The greater power of the Merlin boosted the top speed of the Warhawk to 373 mph and improved the performance dramatically at higher altitudes. This version was distinguishable from the others in the series by the fact that it had no carburettor intake on top of the cowling. A total of 1,311 P-40Fs were built, all apart from the first 260 having a 20-inch longer rear fuselage to improve directional stability at low speed. The aircraft could carry a 170 gallon drop tank or a 500 lb bomb and was known as the Kittyhawk II by the RAF. At least 100 of these aircraft were transferred to the Soviet Union and others went to the Free French Air Force.

In parallel with the P-40F, the K model with an Allison V-1710-73 engine was produced. This, too, was a more powerful version and had a top speed of 360 mph in spite of a greatly increased gross weight. It was the heaviest of the P-40 series and like the 'F' had the 31-foot long fuselage but in addition was equipped with a small dorsal fin which overcame the tendency to swing on take-off. The P-40M was a similar machine in external appearance but had a slightly modified engine.

By now the P-40 had acquired so much extra weight with additional war equipment such as armour and extra fuel that it became necessary to produce a lightweight version. Often known as the 'Gipsy Rose Lee' because it was partly stripped, this machine, the P-40L, had two of the six wing guns removed, some of the armour deleted, fuel capacity lessened and other items modified, saving some 250 lb on the gross weight. It followed the P-40F into production and 700 were built.

The most prolific of all Warhawk variants was the P-40N which occupied the Curtiss production lines from 1943 until terminated a year later. By this time the Allison engine had been increased in power to 1,200 hp and the original version was a lightweight variant with only four wing guns. The top speed was increased to 378 mph at 10,500 feet, but as time went on it was found necessary to bring back the original wing armament which was restored to six .50 inch machine-guns and shackles for a 1,500 lb bomb load were incorporated under the wings and fuselage. It thus became an extremely effective fighter-bomber in both the Middle East and Pacific areas. A total of 1,977 P-40Ns were built and served not only with the USAAF but with Britain, Russia, China, South Africa and Australia. A total of 568 Warhawks of this variant, which the RAF knew as the Kittyhawk IV, equipped several squadrons in Italy whilst the large proportion of all P-40s went to the Soviet Union. Here 2,097 were supplied but they were not very popular with the Russians who considered the aircraft incapable of absorbing as much battle damage as the P-39 Airacobra.

One of the most successful operators of the Warhawk was the Free French. Following the invasion of North Africa in 1942 the local French Air Force squadrons became allies and had their old Hawk 75 fighters replaced by more modern Warhawks. They took a leading part in the ground attack campaign against armour and troop concentrations in Tunisia before the Germans capitulated. The original unit to use the aircraft was GCII/5 which became the *Group Lafayette*.

The Warhawk was also the first aircraft to feature the 'sharks mouth' insignia on the nose. During World War 2 this was probably started by No 112 'Shark' Squadron in the Western Desert, although Chennault's American Volunteer Group in China also used this insignia.

By 1944 it had become painfully obvious that the P-40 was no longer a really effective aircraft in the role it was then carrying out. In all, some 2,500 were on USAAF strength in April 1944 but this dwindled to a single operational group within 12 months. The production lines in America, having been fully geared for war production by that time, were producing sufficient Mustangs and Thunderbolts to be able to re-equip the squadrons with the more modern aircraft and therefore the Warhawk disappeared very rapidly from the scene.

The Warhawk was relegated to operational training and the final production aircraft delivered were three two-seat P-40Ns following the number of conversions made in the field by training establishments to give fledgling fighter pilots an idea of what the machine could do. These aircraft were

P-40K of 23rd Fighter Group (the 'Flying Tigers') in China. Note kill markings beneath canopy (USAAF official).

unofficially known as TP-40Ns and
served until the end of the war.

Curtiss P-40D Warhawk Specification
Type Single-seat fighter-bomber.
Power plant One 1,200 hp Allison
V-1710-81 12-cylinder liquid-cooled
engine.
Performance Max speed 308 mph at
5,000 feet. Range 750 miles. Ceiling
31,000 feet.
Dimensions Span 37 feet 4 inches.
Length 33 feet 4 inches. Height 10 feet
7 inches.
Armament Six .5 inch machine-guns
plus three 500 lb bombs.

Douglas P-70 Havoc

The P-70 Havoc was a development
of the basic A-20 attack bomber for the
USAAC which had a varied career in
both the British and French Air Forces
before being adopted by the Americans. Using its maker's designation
(DB-7), the original aircraft was supplied to the French as a light bomber.
However, the fall of France meant that
orders for 105 examples were taken
over by the RAF and used as the Boston
on daylight raids against the continent
of Europe.

At the same time as the US Army
decided that it needed the Havoc for its
own use, the attacks by the Luftwaffe
on Britain at night set a problem which
was difficult to overcome because
there were no night fighters in existence capable of carrying the primitive
radar then available.

*A rare picture of the P-70 Havoc with
'arrow-head' radar aerials on the nose
following the standard British AI practice. A 20 mm gun pack was included
in the under fuselage position as can
be seen on the second aircraft in the
formation.*

Led by the British conversions and
the various modifications made to the
basic DB-7 airframe, the USAAC
ordered the development of a
specialised night fighter based on the
A-20 design.

The original prototype XP-70 was the
beginning of a contract for a further 59
aircraft which were delivered between
April and September 1942. They were
largely used by training squadrons
awaiting delivery of their Northrop
P-61s and initiated crews in the new art
of radar interception.

The aircraft had a solid nose into
which the radar was installed. Under
the fuselage a gun pack containing
four 20 mm cannon was concentrated.

A further 39 A-20Cs were modified as
P-70A-1s, having six .50 inch
machine-guns in the nose, and 65
A-20Gs were converted as P-70A-2s. A
further experimental version of the
A-20G was equipped with three .50
inch guns in large blisters on each side
of the fuselage to become the only
P-70B-1 example.

The P-70A saw limited service in the
Pacific area but was replaced by the
Northrop P-61 Black Widow in 1944.
The name Havoc, which was first

American Fighters of World War 2

applied to the RAF night fighting version, was adopted by the USAAF for the A-20 attack bomber and equally applied to the P-70.

Douglas P-70 Havoc Specification
Type Two-seat night fighter.
Power plant Two 1,200 hp Pratt & Whitney R-1830-S3C4G Twin Wasp 14-cylinder radial air-cooled engines.
Performance Max speed 295 mph at 13,000 feet. Cruising speed 270 mph. Range 996 miles. Ceiling 25,800 feet.
Dimensions Span 61 feet 4 inches. Length 47 feet. Height 15 feet 10 inches.

Armament Six .50 inch machine-guns or four 20 mm cannon in nose.

Lockheed P-38 Lightning

One of the best-known USAAF fighters operational in World War 2, the P-38 was already in mass production before the war started. In January 1937 the Army Air Corps asked the American aircraft industry to submit designs for a new fighter aircraft capable of interception and attack on enemy aircraft at high altitudes. The specification called for a top speed of

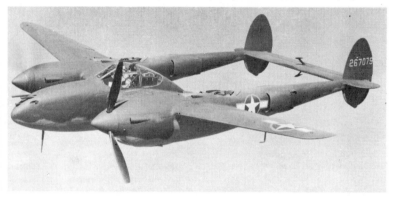

Above *Lockheed P-38H-5-LO, one of the first of the long line of Lightning variants to see active service. This machine was built in 1943. Note the red outline to the national insignia.* **Below** *Radar-equipped, two-seat, night fighting P-38M which saw service in the Pacific in the closing stages of the war and was the fastest night fighter available on the Allied side.*

360 mph and a climb rate from sea level to 20,000 feet of six minutes.

The design chosen was that by Clarence 'Kelly' L. Johnson, the Lockheed chief design engineer. This was Lockheed's Model 22 and a contract was let for one XP-38 aircraft which was eventually serialled 37-457.

The new design was revolutionary for its time. It employed a twin-boom layout with the engines, turbo-superchargers, radiator and main undercarriage units all carried in the booms. At that time the armament of the new aircraft was also somewhat radical. This allowed for one 23 mm and four .50 inch guns in the nose. It was also one of the first American aircraft to

Above *Lockheed P-38G Lightning. A total of 1,082 of this variant were built and saw service in the landings on Sicily and in the Pacific.* **Below** *Lightning Droopsnoot. Developed from a standard P-38L based in the UK, Lockheed engineers redesigned the nose to have a Norden bomb sight so that this type of aircraft could act as lead ship for other bomb-carrying Lightnings in an effort to fool the Luftwaffe. Conversions were made in late 1944.*

American Fighters of World War 2

use a tricycle undercarriage configuration, and with a gross weight of 14,800 lb was heavier than some of the contemporary bombers.

The prototype was constructed in great secrecy. However, as soon as the prototype aircraft left the production line misfortune began plaguing it. During the first taxi test the brakes failed and on January 27 1939 during the first flight from March Field, Lieutenant B. S. Kelsey, the pilot, had to make an emergency landing with the flaps retracted after one of the linkages had broken.

Two weeks after the first flight, on February 11 1939 the XP-38 was delivered across the continent to Mitchell Field taking seven hours two minutes and two refuelling stops to make the journey. This almost set a new American record and the 2,400 mile journey was accomplished at an average speed of 340 mph. Then misfortune struck again. Unfortunately Kelsey throttled the engines back to lower the troublesome landing flaps to avoid overshooting Mitchell Field and when he attempted to accelerate the engines they would not respond. The XP-38 crashed on to a golf course just short of the runway and was destroyed.

Despite this unfortunate accident the aircraft had demonstrated a spectacular performance and 13 pre-production YP-38s were ordered by the Army Air Corps on April 27 1939, whilst on August 10 1939 a full production contract was awarded to Lockheed. This called for an initial 66 examples and was followed by another for 607. The production line was established at Burbank, California, and the first 30 aircraft were completed as P-38s similar to the pre-production prototypes by then in service.

The first YP-38 had flown on September 16 1940 and was delivered to the USAAC in March 1941 for evaluation. The whole batch was completed by June of that year and the production aircraft followed almost immediately.

Certain modifications, such as an alteration in the tailplane incidence to overcome a buffeting problem, and the addition of self-sealing fuel tanks, were introduced in the light of European combat experience.

The aircraft was, however, rather slow to enter service. Many of the earlier versions, including the pre-production batch, were used for experimental purposes.

In November 1941 the P-38E started to come from the Burbank production line and was distinguishable by having a 20 mm Hispano cannon in the nose and provision for greater ammunition capacity.

No Lightnings were available in squadron service at the time of the Japanese attack on Pearl Harbour on December 7 1941. It was only then that production gathered pace and almost nine months after the outbreak of war before a P-38D shot down its first enemy aircraft. This occurred over the North Atlantic on the morning of August 14 1942 when Lieutenant Elza Shahan of the 27th Fighter Squadron, 1st Fighter Group, destroyed a Focke-Wulf Fw200 reconnaissance aircraft shadowing an allied convoy. The Lightning was based in Iceland together with a number of Bell P-39s which also took part in the engagement. Lieutenant Shahan was awarded the Silver Star Medal for his part in the action and he became the first Lightning pilot to score a victory against the Luftwaffe in the European theatre of operations.

The Lightning was one of the many aircraft ordered by the British Purchasing Commission in 1941 and requirements for 667 aircraft were made known. Out of these 143 were built but only three reached Britain early in 1942 for evaluation. All of the others were repossessed by the USAAF after America's entry into the war. A further 524 aircraft on British contract were also absorbed into the American Forces and none reached the UK.

The P-38F followed the 'E' into production at Burbank early in 1942. This had 1,325 hp Allison V-1710-49/53 engines and for the first time had racks under the inner wings for either 2,000 lb of bombs, torpedoes or 310 gallon drop tanks. Another modification on this version was what was then known as the 'manoeuvring flap'. This allowed the Fowler landing flaps to be extended eight degrees at combat speed to increase the wing lift and therefore the manoeuvrability. P-38Fs were also the first Lightnings to be used as two-seat trainers. The pupil was crammed into a small space behind the instructor in place of the radio equipment in order to gain an impression of handling and fighter tactics. Production totalled 527 aircraft and was followed by 1,082 P-38Gs which were externally similar, differing only in equipment changes.

As the availability of the Lightning became better the first Fighter Groups to cross the Atlantic for operations in England began. The first groups selected were the 1st and 14th and they also became the first to fly the Atlantic direct instead of going as deck cargo by sea. Of the 186 P-38Gs sent, 179 arrived safely after stops in Labrador, Greenland and Iceland. This long-range ability of the Lightning saved months of precious time and allowed pilots to reach combat readiness long before the time it would have taken had the aircraft been shipped by conventional transport methods. Once in England the two groups trained for combat operations over Europe and were employed on coastal patrol work, fighter sweeps and some bomber escort work, though on a limited basis.

Only a few combat missions were undertaken before these P-38s were sent to North Africa in support of the Anglo-American invasion of November 1942. A number of P-38s of the 82nd Fighter Group were also flown to North Africa via the Atlantic, flying parallel to the European coast to arrive in North Africa after the initial landings had taken place.

In action against German fighters for the first time, Lightnings gained the German nickname of 'The Fork-tailed Devil' but in fact did not prove as successful as was hoped in fighter-to-fighter combat operations. It was found that the P-38's manoeuvrability at low level was distinctly lacking and the Bf 109s and Fw 190s could run rings round them at tree-top level. They did, however, have the advantage of long range, and it was using this capability that the Lightning really proved its worth in the North African campaign. When used against the hundreds of lumbering Junkers Ju 52s attempting to supply Rommel's forces by air, the Lightning proved its worth. Its ability to be able to seek out and destroy these aircraft contributed greatly to the early end of the North African campaign. They later participated in the invasion of Sicily and Italy and continued in service until the end of the war.

Whereas the Lightning did not gain tremendous fame in Europe as an air-to-air combat fighter, it had far better success in the Pacific Theatre. Once again, its long range enabled it to bring the battle to the enemy. The first Lightnings entered service in the Pacific area late in 1942. P-38Gs based on Guadalcanal in April 1943 were notable for an operation which caught the imagination of the public at that time. Pilots from the 12th, 70th and 339th Fighter Squadrons intercepted Admiral Yamamoto's aircraft and escort 550 miles from their base in a spectacular operation. This was due to the Americans having cracked the Japanese radio codes allowing them to know the Admiral's movements at the same time as the Japanese did themselves. It is doubtful if this action and the death of Yamamoto significantly changed the course of the war, but it added greatly to the prestige of the Lightning and to the morale of Allied fighter pilots in the area.

The very first Lightning unit in the South Pacific was a flight of F-4s of the 8th Photographic Reconnaissance Squadron. These were camera-equipped variants of the P-38 which were used successfully in all theatres of operation. Led by Major Carl Poliska, they arrived at Port Moresby in April 1942. The high speed and altitude of the F-4s provided them with almost complete freedom from interception and thus allied intelligence gained greatly from their activities. This unit was later attached to the 6th Reconnaissance Group which flew the later version, the F-5, from New Guinea, the Philippines and Okinawa. The first P-38Fs arrived in Australia late in 1942 and after modifications were assigned to one squadron each of the 35th and 49th Fighter Groups. They met with considerable success, shooting down over 20 enemy aircraft for no loss to themselves.

The only entire Lightning-equipped group in the south west Pacific was the 475th which was part of the 5th Air Force and also included the 8th and 347th Fighter Groups, some of which were equipped with this aircraft. In the 13th Air Force the 18th Fighter Group and the 4th Reconnaissance Group had Lightning squadrons, and the 7th Air Force in the Central Pacific had but one P-38 unit. In the Aleutians the 51st and 80th Fighter Groups together with the 8th Reconnaissance Group formed the large majority of the fighters operating in this area.

Major Richard Bong, who flew with the 9th Fighter Squadron, became the leading American ace in the last war with 40 victories. He is credited with having said that the P-38 was the best fighter in the Pacific and certainly proved his words. Bong was closely followed by Major Thomas McGuire who had 38 victories, again all scored while flying the Lightning.

Like the Germans, the Japanese Air Force described the P-38 in its own way. Japanese pilots saw the American machine as 'two aeroplanes with one pilot' and its long range and heavy armament contributed greatly to the high scores.

Most of all P-38 models up to the H had streamlined engine cowlings. An obvious change of outline came, however, when the P-38J introduced chin radiators under the spinners. The engines were V-1710-89/91s and the 'J' had its internal fuel tankage increased and hydraulic power boosting for the ailerons. With 410 gallons of internal fuel and two 300 gallon drop tanks, the Lightning now had a total ferry endurance of 12 hours and a combat radius sufficient to escort the 8th Air Force bombers in Europe on deep penetration raids into Germany.

The final 'fighter' Lightning was the P-38L. It was also the most numerously built and possibly the most important variant of this aircraft. Externally similar to the 'J' model, 3,810 were built by Lockheed and a further 113 by Vultee at Nashville.

In Europe the Lightning was used on an increasing scale for ground attack and fighter bomber work. The P-38L was modified to carry rocket projectiles in 'Christmas Tree' tiers under the wings. During the invasion of Europe the Lightning was assigned the low-level fighter protection task of the invasion fleet, mainly because its twin boom configuration was easy to recognise and the chance of false identification by trigger-happy gunners was lessened.

The use of the Lightning as a ground-attack aircraft was supplemented by its ability as a high-level bomber. Several aircraft of the 9th Air Force in Britain were modified to take the famous Norden bomb sight in a transparent nose. These machines carried a bombardier and flew in the lead of a group of Lightnings on high level carpet bombing operations. Once over the target all the aircraft in the formation released their bombs on a signal from the bombardier and thereafter were able to give a good account of themselves should they be attacked by enemy fighters.

With the bombardier nose the Lightning gained the nickname of 'droopsnoot' and was followed by another version using BTO (bomb-through-overcast) radar in a bulbous nose.

Following experiments with twin seats in the Lightning for training purposes, Lockheed were asked to develop a radar-equipped night fighter version of the P-38L, which was produced in the late stages of the war. The P-38M, as it was called, reached operational status in the Pacific and had an observer in a raised seat

behind the pilot, which altered the outline shape of the central nacelle. The radar was fitted in a pod under the nose and although only 75 of these aircraft were converted they were 50 mph faster than the P-61 Black Widow and just as effective.

In an attempt to develop the Lightning even further, Lockheed produced the XP-58 Chain Lightning which was an enlarged two-seater fighter development of the P-38, and although a single prototype (41-2670) was built and flown in June 1944 it was not produced in quantity. This machine had a four-gun turret in addition to an interchangeable nose armament of one 75 mm cannon or two 20 mm and four .50 inch machine-guns. It had a maximum speed of 430 mph and continued the line of heavy escort fighters started by the Lightning.

Of the three principal USAAF fighters used during World War 2, the Lightning can easily be described as the most versatile. It was used in all theatres of war, capable of landing on the snow in Iceland and in the heat of the south west Pacific jungles. It could carry torpedoes, bombs or be adapted for photo-reconnaissance work.

Lockheed P-38L Lightning
Specification
Type Single-seat long-range fighter, fighter-bomber and night fighter.
Power plant Two 1,225 hp Allison V-1710-49/53 12-cylinder liquid-cooled in-line engines.
Performance Max speed 347 mph at 5,000 feet. Range (internal fuel) 400 miles. Ceiling 39,000 feet.

Dimensions Span 52 feet. Length 37 feet 10 inches. Height 9 feet 10 inches.
Armament One 20 mm Hispano cannon and four .50 inch machine-guns in the nose plus maximum of two 1,000 lb bombs, rockets or fuel tanks.

North American P-51 Mustang

The Mustang was unique. It was one of the very few Allied aircraft types that were designed after the start of World War 2 yet saw almost unlimited service in every theatre of operations. The most surprising thing of all is that the aircraft was nearly a non-starter with the American air force as it owed its origin to a British requirement for a fighter, better than those that other American companies could offer at the time of the Battle of Britain.

It is also surprising that such a perfect aircraft was designed and built by a company which had almost no experience of fighter aircraft design. The British Purchasing Commission under the auspices of Sir Henry Self, a distinguished Civil Servant, operated from offices in New York and one of their top priorities was to obtain the best possible single-seat fighters to supplement the Spitfires and Hurricanes which at that time were giving such a good account of themselves against the Luftwaffe.

The original British choice was for the Curtiss P-40. This machine however, powered by an Allison liquid-cooled engine, gave a very poor performance over 15,000 feet and the RAF was calling for an aircraft which could operate at altitudes above this.

The Purchasing Commission knew well that their choice, although adequate for several roles, did not fill the most pressing requirements, and therefore when North American offered the B-25 bomber it was thought that they might entertain the idea of producing a fighter of their own design but with strict regard to the British requirements.

Time was the overriding consideration, as the RAF could not wait long for large quantities of the proposed new aircraft. North American suggested that they could design a single-seater fighter around the same Allison engine used by the Curtiss machines, and obtain superior performance through an extremely low-drag airframe. The construction would be developed in such a way that mass production techniques to facilitate rapid manufacture could be used.

Previously, Sir Henry Self had dealt with 'Dutch' Kindelberger of North American and had been suitably

The red and yellow chequers round the nose and similar colours on the spinner identify this P-51D as belonging to the 357th Fighter Group, 363rd Fighter Squadron, based at Leiston, Suffolk. The fin is red and the aircraft is named 'Love of mine'.

impressed by the way in which the company had produced Harvard trainers for the RAF. In spite of the general lack of design experience, North American engineers under Raymond Rice and Edgar Schmued accepted a 120 day limit for the construction of a prototype which was by then known as the NA-73X.

In keeping with their promise, North American used a laminar-flow wing section, an aft-mounted ventral radiator for minimum drag, and simple lines for easy manufacture.

Bearing the civil registration NX19998, the first machine was rolled out at Inglewood, California, 117 days after work on the design had been started. Shortly afterwards a 1100 hp Allison V-1710-F3R engine was installed and the aircraft flew for the first time on October 25 1940. Production began immediately and the first aircraft came off the line before the end of 1941.

In the interim period between the first flight of the prototype and that of the first production aircraft, North American ran into the usual snags that an experimental aircraft can expect. After the first few flights it was revealed that the Allison engine tended to overheat, indicating that the cooling had to be greatly improved. However, disaster struck on the fifth flight of the prototype when the engine cut as the aircraft was coming in to land, and in attempting a dead stick landing the pilot, Vance Breese,

ended up with the machine on its back having sustained major damage.

Luckily, enough hours had been accumulated before the accident for the British Purchasing Commission to have confidence in the design. It had already been proved that the aircraft was superior to other US-built fighter types and therefore a preliminary production order was placed for 300 machines. This was shortly increased to 620 and by the end of the production run more than 15,000 Mustangs had been built.

By allowing North American to undertake this work for a foreign air force, the USAAC made the bargain that two examples of the production model should be supplied free of charge for evaluation by their own pilots. The fourth and tenth production machines were sent to Wright Field where they were tested under the designation XP-51.

Rather surprisingly they were employed in testing special items of equipment and not immediately evaluated to meet service requirements. It appeared that the Army had 'taken its pound of flesh' and thereafter had very little interest in acquiring models for its own use.

North American Aviation were equally surprised and it is reputed that only the personal intervention of General Arnold secured the acceptance of the Mustang by the USAAF for its own use.

Originally the name 'Apache' was adopted for the American version, which differed from British Mustangs by having an armament of four 20 mm cannon in the wings replacing the four .30 inch, two .50 inch wing guns and two .50 inch fuselage guns of the earlier model.

These alterations complicated the supply of the aircraft to the RAF. With the introduction of Lease-Lend it was necessary for either the USAAF or USN to order the same aircraft before they could be supplied to other powers. It therefore meant that 150 cannon-armed Mustang IAs were ordered by the British in September 1941 in order to keep arrangements respectable.

Matters changed considerably on December 7 1941 when, due to the Japanese attack, the Americans suddenly became allies rather than supporters of the British cause. The result was that the USAAF looked around hurriedly to increase aircraft production in order to meet almost unbelievable requirements in the field.

The original P-51s were modified to take underwing bombs and were fitted with airbrakes for use as dive bombers. The Americans believed that by

The P-51H was a post-war variant known as the 'lightweight' Mustang because of the almost total redesign of the airframe. In this picture can be seen the different shape of the undercarriage, taller fin and rudder, deeper fuselage and altered air intake configuration (Harry Walker).

American Fighters of World War 2

'The Impatient Virgin', coded L2:Z and belonging to the 479th Fighter Group, 434th Fighter Squadron, probably based at Wattisham. The rudder was painted red.

adapting the machine in this way it would have a vastly superior performance to its contemporaries and be suitable for operations then being planned.

Given the designation A-36A, the first aircraft came off the Inglewood production line in September 1942, but although these machines were used in a limited way in North Africa they met with no great success. Even so the USAAF placed a contract for 1,200 P-51s, modifying the armament to include all .50 inch machine-guns instead of cannon.

The 86th Bomb Group with four squadrons was the first A-36A-trained unit employed overseas, sailing for North Africa in March 1943. Just over 300 A-36As were available by that time and they took part in the attack on the enemy-held island of Pantellaria followed by the invasion of Sicily.

Another A-36 Group to see combat was the 311th, which went to India by way of Australia in July 1943. About 40 aircraft were available in two squadrons and they were used for tactical combat operations, reconnaissance, strafing, dive-bombing and patrol work.

Although the range of the Mustang was good, it was found that this could be supplemented by the addition of long-range fuel tanks which produced the possibility of 2,000 miles plus. This range was far in excess of that available in any other fighters then serving in the European or Pacific theatres of war. Other modifications were made by the RAF who, on requesting 'more power', produced one aircraft powered by a Rolls-Royce Merlin at the instigation of Ronald Harker, then a Rolls-Royce test pilot.

A two-stage two-speed supercharged Merlin 61 was adapted to fit the Mustang. It surprisingly gave a 70 mph advantage over the Allison Mustang's maximum and the altitude performance was greatly improved at a height of 25,000 feet. This proved to be better than the current Spitfire at that time and plans were made to manufacture the Merlin in the US at the Packard factory in Detroit.

The first Merlin-powered Mustang was flown on October 13 1942 and after preliminary modifications had been made to the prototype, AL975, full details were sent to America with the British Air Staff's recommendation.

The North American design team at Inglewood were surprised at the ease with which they could squeeze the Merlin into the existing engine mounting with so few alterations. The external appearance of the aircraft changed little as the major alteration was confined to moving the air intake (previously on top of the nose) to the underside and combining the intercooler radiator with that of the main coolant radiator in the ventral scoop. In fact this alteration gave the Mustang an even more streamlined appearance and enhanced its top speed capabilities. The XP-51B, to give the new aircraft its eventual title, made its initial flight on November 30 1942 with test pilot Robert Chilton in command. Apart from minor hitches the test programme went well and an order for Merlin Mustangs was approved on December 28 1942. It was not, however, until June 1943 that production of this variant came from the Inglewood factory, while in August that year the new North American factory at Dallas, Texas, was turned over to Mustang production.

October 1943 was one of the worst times for the US air forces committed to the strategic bombing of German industry. At that time the loss rate was nearing ten per cent and it was touch and go as to whether the offensive would be continued. Both Thunderbolts and Lightnings had been used on long range escort missions with the bombers, but their performance was not sufficiently good to keep off the attacking German fighters.

A new unit was selected to take the Mustang into combat in the ETO. This was the 354th Fighter Group, which went to Boxted airfield near Colchester in mid-November 1943. It was immediately thrown into the battle after operational exercises and Major Donald Blakeslee, a veteran of the RAF Eagle Squadrons, was appointed to lead.

The 8th Air Force was intent on making the maximum use of the P-51B's range and by December 11 enough 75 gallon drop tanks were available to enable the Mustangs to accompany the bombers as far as Emden on a mission.

Several escorted raids were carried out before the new fighter scored its first victory. This came on December 16 when Lieutenant Charles F. Gumm of the 355th Fighter Squadron shot down a Me110 over Bremen, to be followed four days later by three further claims by other pilots. Unfortunately, on the debit side three American fighters failed to return making a total of five missing in action in six missions. As far as was known all of these were due to mechanical failure. At the height at which the P-51B had to fly various mechanical malfunctions made themselves apparent. Wind shield heating proved insufficient and often frost obscured vision; coolant leaks occurred and spark plugs quickly fouled up due to the retarded engine setting necessary to conserve fuel on the long flight in the company of bombers. Persistent jamming of the guns during combat was also encountered during tight turns, and modifications had to be made to the ammunition belts which were causing the trouble.

In spite of these technical difficulties in early 1944, the 354th gained experience rapidly and modified their tactics to suit operational conditions. On January 5 they all but eliminated a bunch of Me110s over Kiel claiming 18 enemy aircraft destroyed for no losses to themselves. Six days later 15 planes were credited for no losses during furious battles in the vicinity of Oschersleben and Halberstadt.

February also marked the operational debut of a second Mustang Group, the 357th, which was based at Leiston, Suffolk. This Group and the 363rd, together with the original 354th, comprised the newly formed 9th Air Force's Mustang force. The 8th Air Force, unable to get Mustangs until later, settled for the untried 357th Group at the end of January.

Meanwhile, the Mustang continued in service with the RAF experiencing similar problems in its operational use. No 65 Squadron pilots complained about the lack of visibility and restricted headroom in the Mustang cockpit. Their contemporaries had for a long time been using the bulbous one-piece sliding canopy on the Spitfire, and to overcome the problem a Mustang was fitted experimentally at Boscombe Down with a canopy of this type.

Nearly all RAF Mustang IIIs were eventually fitted with these canopies — known as Malcolm Hoods after the designer — and a great many also went into service with the USAAF in Europe.

More and more Mustangs continued to arrive in the ETO. The third Group, the 363rd based at Rivenhall, Essex, became operational on February 22 and by the 25th of that month the 8th Air Force's oldest unit (the 4th Fighter Group at Debden, Essex) converted. This group became the star performer with the Mustang and amassed a considerable number of victories as well as colourful personalities. Pilots like Duane Beeson and Don Gentile, who had started their combat experience on Spitfires, soon became high-scoring aces in only a few weeks of intense operations.

The 4th Fighter Group went on to destroy 1,000 enemy aircraft by the end of the war and Major John T. Godfrey claimed 36 aircraft destroyed whilst Don Gentile came second with 30.

Round trips of 1,200 miles were now becoming commonplace and the Luftwaffe was facing a fighter of ability equal to their own Messerschmitts and Focke-Wulfs anywhere over Germany.

Following the Malcolm Hood on the P-51C, the complete bubble-canopied six-gun Mustang reached combat squadrons in England during May 1944. The first machines went to Group and squadron commanders for whom the better view from the cockpit was an added aid in keeping an eye on their own formations and opposing enemy forces.

This version of the Mustang was the famous P-51D which additionally had a strengthened wing allowing much heavier loads of external fuel or bombs to be carried, as by now the Mustang was being used to range further and further into Germany on ground-attack missions after having escorted the bombers to their target.

This ground strafing was a dangerous practice as most German airfields were heavily defended by light anti-aircraft guns, making life hazardous for the unwary or unskilled.

The USAAF re-equipped all but one of its 15 Fighter Groups with the 'D' model, totalling 42 Squadrons. In all 1,500 aircraft, constituting by far and away the largest force of Mustangs operating in any theatre during World War 2, contributed greatly to final victory.

The first Merlin-powered Mustangs were not used against the Japanese in the Far East until 1944 when these aircraft were shipped to India to supplement Allison-powered versions. By April of that year the 311th Group near the Burmese border received the first examples and others went to the 14th Air Force in China.

One of the many P-51Ds given by the Americans to the South Koreans when their air force was formed during the Korean war (Aviation Photo News).

The P-51D did not see great service in the Pacific, however, until its long range was particularly needed to escort B-29s on their bombing attacks against industrial and military targets in Japan itself.

Two Fighter Groups, the 15th and 21st, were sent to Iwo Jima in March 1945 for this purpose.

By the time Japan was beaten in August 1945 the Americans had 5,500 Mustangs in service, whilst the RAF and Commonwealth air forces had another 1,300.

The end of the war saw the rapid rundown of fighter groups in the same way that other American forces returned to the States for deactivation. It was not so easy, however, to get rid of the Mustang itself, and the many surplus aircraft were sold or given to developing air forces of the liberated countries and were also used by Air National Guard units in the United States itself. Between May 1946 and December 1948 ANG squadrons received 700 surplus P-51Ds and a further four squadrons were given the tactical reconnaissance version which were by then known as RF-51Ds.

By 1952 68 out of a total of 98 ANG squadrons were operating Mustangs before changing over to more modern jet aircraft.

Others were sold to the air forces of Sweden, Italy, France, Switzerland, Israel, Canada, New Zealand, the Philippines and many Latin American countries. Others were flown by the Nationalist Chinese in their civil war against the communists and retired to Formosa when Chiang Kai Chek's forces left the mainland.

In Australia the Mustang was manufactured under licence by the government aircraft factory at Port Melbourne, several being equipped with British-built Merlins rather than the American version. The Dutch used the Mustang against Nationalist rebels in Indonesia before that country became an independent state, and when the North Koreans invaded South Korea the Mustang once again came into its own.

This, however, is another story, and outside the limits of this book. Sufficient to say that the Mustang was one of the most famous and well-liked fighter aircraft ever to be produced.

This story would not be complete without mention of the various experimental versions of the Mustang that were built. Perhaps the most interesting of these was the XP-51F 'lightweight' Mustang, three of which were produced as interceptors in 1944. The first flew on February 14 1944 and was essentially a completely redesigned Mustang, although the external shape was virtually the same.

The aerodynamics were considerably improved and gave the aircraft a 20 mile an hour increase in top speed using the same engine as the 'D' model. The cockpit hood was much larger and better blended into the fuselage line. Similarly, the under-belly radiator was redesigned and the undercarriage lightened with smaller wheels.

Another version, the 'G' had a five-bladed Rotol airscrew, giving it a top speed of 472 mph at 20,750 feet. Although both versions were tested neither was put into production.

Another Mustang variant was the P-51H. This incorporated the drag-reducing, weight-paring technical modifications of the two previous versions and was developed as an escort fighter incorporating a larger internal fuel load and modified engine.

The 'H' followed the 'D' on the production lines and the first of 555 to be delivered was produced in January 1945. All further contracts after the initial deliveries were cancelled as the war ended.

The final model in the Mustang line was the P-51L, which was essentially the same as the 'H' but with the engine producing no less than 2,270 hp at low level. A two-seat trainer, the TP-51M-NT, was also built, but all of these projects were cancelled after the production of prototypes.

North American P-51D Specification

Type Single-seat long-range escort fighter.

Power plant One 1,450 hp Rolls-Royce/Packard Merlin V-1650-7 in-line engine.

American Fighters of World War 2

One of the first 200 Black Widows which had the four-gun top turret deleted because of buffeting (W. T. Larkins).

Performance Max speed 437 mph at 25,000 feet. Range with external fuel 2,080 miles. Ceiling 40,000 feet.
Dimensions Span 37 feet. Length 32 feet 3 inches. Height 13 feet 8 inches.
Armament Six .50 inch machine-guns and up to 2,000 lb bombs or ten 5-inch rocket projectiles under wings.

Northrop P-61 Black Widow

The experience of the British during the night attacks on London and other industrial centres in Britain during 1940 and '41 led the USAAC to hurriedly look for a suitable night fighter aircraft capable of carrying a heavy offensive armament and the bulky radar equipment then being introduced. As in so many other areas of combat aircraft the Americans were totally unprepared to meet night attacks and therefore production had to be initiated rapidly in order to combat the potential menace.

The Northrop company offered a twin-engined twin-boom aeroplane in November 1940 which was large enough to carry all the equipment needed and had room for crewmen to operate it as well as sufficient range and armament.

Two prototypes of this design were ordered as the XP-61 on January 11 1941, and the first prototype flew for the first time on May 26 1942. Development flying was concentrated on 13 YP-61s, the orders for which were placed in March 1941, to be followed by 150 production aircraft and a subsequent contract for 410 placed in February 1942.

In all a total of 575 prototype and production aircraft were built by Northrop and they were used in both the Pacific and European war zones.

The first prototype was finished in natural metal overall and powered by two Pratt & Whitney R-2800-10, 18-cylinder, radial engines driving Hamilton Standard propellers. The prototype was fitted with a mock-up turret above the fuselage to contain four .50 inch machine-guns before the delivery of the actual General Electric unit. The first flight lasted 15 minutes, during which test pilot Vance Breese concluded that the aircraft would eventually become a winner. A number of modifications had to be made, however, including a change in the horizontal tail surfaces to improve longitudinal stability. The wing trailing edge was also rebuilt to incorporate full span flaps and ailerons.

These modifications were built into the second prototype, XP-61, during its construction, and the machine flew for the first time on November 18 1942.

The first of 200 P-61As appeared towards the end of 1943. Difficulties because of buffeting were encountered with the top turret and after the 37th production machine, this was deleted. The 46th production aircraft also had an engine change installing R-2800-65 units which added extra horsepower.

The 13 pre-production aircraft were used for numerous night fighting experiments. One of these was concerned with the colour scheme to be

The P-61A's gloss black finish is shown to advantage in this factory-fresh model. Note that in this view the top gun turret with its four .50 inch machine-guns has been retained.

used on operational machines and in a series of tests three Black Widows were painted either natural metal, olive green or gloss black. All three were tested against searchlight beams by flying through a concentration of them during the tests. The gloss black machine was not seen at all, though the others stood out quite distinctly. It was because of this that all subsequent production aircraft were painted gloss black overall and the name 'Black Widow' was adopted.

The P-61 entered service in both the Pacific and European theatres of operations during the early summer of 1944. Before this, however, the existence of the aircraft was effectively leaked by a drawing appearing in a comic strip in a US newspaper. The existence of the Black Widow was quickly revealed after this incident, which was picked up by a number of American and British aviation publications.

The first units to operate the P-61 in Europe were the 422nd and 425th night fighter squadrons of the 9th Air Force, which took delivery of their machines in May 1944 and were subsequently used on the Continent for night fighter operations. They ranged far into Germany at night and hit enemy raiders over allied lines. Other offensive operations were organised against enemy mechanised

transport, troop columns, supplies and aircraft on the ground. The first victory for a P-61 pilot over Europe was credited to Lieutenant Raymond A. Anderson and subsequently Lieutenant Paul A. Smith became the first Black Widow ace when he shot down five enemy aircraft at night.

However, only a limited number of Black Widows were available for operations and these were frequently unserviceable due to problems with their radar equipment and other mechanical failures. They took part in the Battle of the Bulge and the 422nd Squadron won a Distinguished Unit Citation for their part. Later both European-based squadrons were involved in shooting down flying bombs at night during attacks on Antwerp.

The first kill credited to a USAAF pilot in the south Pacific area went to a pilot of the 18th Fighter Group which included the 419th and 547th Night Fighter Squadrons. These operated over Guadalcanal, New Guinea and the Philippines.

In the latter campaign Japanese aircraft, which were denied freedom of

American Fighters of World War 2

operation during the day as their airfields were swamped by attacks from American fighters, started night intruder operations against American forces. The Black Widow was an effective counter against these and Major Carroll C. Smith of the 547th Night Fighter Squadron became the first Black Widow ace in the Pacific. He destroyed four Japanese aircraft in a single night, bringing his total score to seven. Black Widows were also used over Saipan where they protected the B-29 airfields from Japanese night attack.

In July 1944 the first of 450 P-61Bs were produced. This version could carry four 1,600 lb bombs under the wings or, alternatively, 300 gallon long-range fuel tanks. The final 250 of this batch had the dorsal turret restored as the stability problems were overcome.

The final production batch comprised 41 P-61Cs with 2,800 hp R-2800-73 engines.

As the Black Widow was conceived at a time when effective night fighter tactics had yet to be evolved, and when radar was in its infancy, it did surprisingly well against its German and Japanese adversaries. The combined firepower of .50 inch machine-guns and four 20 mm cannon was sufficient to knock down any opposing fighter or bomber aircraft.

Forerunner of the famous Thunderbolt, the P-43 Lancer shows the distinctive family resemblance of deep fuselage, radial engine and elliptical wings. It did not see much active service during World War 2 (P. M. Bowers).

Few variants of the basic airframe were built, though out of the P-61 Northrop developed a photo reconnaissance aircraft known as the F-15A Reporter. The idea originated in an experimental cockpit conversion in which a bubble canopy was provided and the two crew members sat in tandem. A total of 36 examples were built in 1946 and the aircraft was redesignated RF-61C in 1948. All of the machines were out of service by 1952.

Northrop P-61 Black Widow Specification
Type Two/three-seat night fighter and intruder aircraft.
Power plant Two 2,250 hp Pratt & Whitney R-2800-65 Double Wasp radial air-cooled engines.
Performance Max speed 330 mph at sea level. Range with external fuel 1,900 miles. Ceiling 33,100 feet.
Dimensions Span 66 feet. Length 48 feet 11 inches. Height 14 feet 2 inches.
Armament Four 20 mm cannon and four .50 inch machine-guns in a dorsal turret (deleted on some models) plus four or six 1,000 lb or 1,600 lb bombs under wings.

Republic P-43 Lancer

In 1935 two aircraft were evaluated by the USAAC to become the first low-wing, retractable undercarriage fighters with enclosed cockpits to see service with the American forces. These were the P-36 and the Seversky P-35. The latter entered limited service with the Army but one aircraft was converted as the XP-41 and fitted with a turbo-supercharged engine for evaluation purposes. As a result of these tests Republic, who had taken over from the Seversky company, developed a slightly improved model which was ordered by the USAAC in 1940 to extend the evaluation period and also to act as an aerodynamic prototype for a trials batch of 13 YP-43s.

The elliptical shape of the P-35's wing was retained but the undercarriage retracted inward instead of towards the rear. Its turbo supercharger gave it a considerable advantage in high altitude operations, which was one of the most important factors in the Army's decision to buy the aircraft.

A contract for 54 was placed in 1940 and deliveries began in 1941. These were the only P-43s to be produced, but after a further evaluation at Wright Field with another Republic aeroplane, the P-44, the Army transferred its order to the latter machine and went on to order another 80.

The war in Europe, however, meant that fighter production in the United States had to be stepped up and another contract was issued for the P-43A in 1941, which had a later engine variant and required a further 125 to be built. The four-gun armament was removed from the nose and placed in the wing. This version of the Lancer had a top speed of 360 mph but did not see active service with the USAAC. In 1942 some were converted to the reconnaissance role with cameras in the rear fuselage. Several machines did see active service against the Japanese as they were delivered to the Chinese Nationalists Forces under Lease-Lend in 1943.

The Lancer had an insignificant career but its successor, the P-47 Thunderbolt, which was developed from it, went on to be one of the most famous fighters of World War 2.

Republic P-43 Lancer Specification
Type Single-seat interceptor fighter.
Power plant One 1,200 hp Pratt &

Whitney R-1830-47 radial air-cooled engine.
Performance Max speed 349 mph at 25,000 feet. Cruising speed 280 mph. Ceiling 38,000 feet. Range 800 miles.
Dimensions Span 36 feet. Length 28 feet 6 inches. Height 14 feet.
Armament Two .50 inch and two .30 inch machine-guns firing forward.

Republic P-47 Thunderbolt

One of the three most outstanding American fighters of World War 2 was the P-47 Thunderbolt. It started Republic's line of fighter-bomber aircraft ending with the F-105 Thunderchief, all of which were successful designs. The P-47 grew out of Seversky's P-35 and P-43. Like its contemporary the P-51 Mustang, the Thunderbolt was conceived, designed and produced entirely within the period 1941-45. It was also the last radial-engined fighter to serve in quantity with the USAAF, although interestingly enough the original design was centred round an in-line Allison engine which was put forward in competition for a specification issued in 1940.

As the heaviest single-seat, single-engine fighter to enter quantity pro-

The first production version of the Thunderbolt was the P-47B, the prototype of which is illustrated here. It was test flown for the first time in May 1941.

American Fighters of World War 2

The tear-drop canopied version of the P-47D Thunderbolt was the most numerous in the European theatre. It was also the heaviest fighter on the Allied side and could take a great deal of damage from enemy fire.

duction (it weighed a little over 12,000 lb) the Thunderbolt utilised the 2,000 hp available in the Pratt & Whitney R-2800 radial engine to provide its power. The first flight of the prototype (40-3051) was made on May 6 1941. The design incorporated a very deep fuselage with a duct from below the engine to the supercharger at the rear. Its elliptical wing plan form was distinctive and it had a massive undercarriage to allow ground clearance for the large-diameter four-bladed propeller. The armament of eight .50 machine-guns in the wings was amongst the heaviest ever conceived for a fighter. It followed the trend of eight-gun fighters in Europe and was retained throughout the aircraft's service.

Problems were encountered in the flight test programme in that when all guns were fired simultaneously the stresses and loads on the wing made necessary a lot of strengthening. The ailerons tended to freeze at altitudes above 30,000 feet and control loads became excessive. Metal control surfaces with balanced trim tabs were adopted to overcome these problems, and a sliding cockpit canopy supplanted the hinged variety in production versions. First models left the assembly line in March 1942 and the first unit to receive the fighter was the 56th Fighter Group which began to re-equip in July 1942.

This was followed by the 78th Fighter Group that joined the 8th Air Force in the UK in 1943.

The P-47B went into action for the first time on April 8 1943 escorting B-17s on near-distance raids and also undertaking fighter sweeps over occupied France. Problems with climb and manoeuvrability were experienced with the early Thunderbolts but it was soon discovered that the aircraft's excellent diving performance and ability to withstand heavy punishment from anti-aircraft fire and enemy fighters stood it in good stead. These early sorties also brought to light the need for the aircraft to carry more fuel if escort missions were to be flown on deep penetration raids into Germany itself.

Many of these problems were overcome with the next variant, the P-47C, that left the Farmingdale, Long Island, production line. Provision was made for a 200 gallon drop tank under the fuselage and other changes included a 13-inch lengthening of the fuselage to improve manoeuvrability. Most of the 602 Thunderbolts built to this specification went to Europe and were flying long range escort missions by the middle of 1943.

The next Thunderbolt to be produced, the P-47D, was also one of the most successful in service. Water injection was added to boost engine power at higher altitudes and this gave the machine a top speed of 433 mph at 30,000 feet.

Originally the Thunderbolt had a sliding canopy which greatly restricted the pilot's view during combat manoeuvres. With the introduction

of the P-47D a new bubble-type canopy was introduced allowing all-round vision, similar to that which previously had been installed on the British Hawker Typhoon. In fact, the first Thunderbolt to be modified used a Typhoon canopy on a cut-down rear fuselage to prove the feasibility of the modification. Once accepted they were promptly introduced onto the P-47D production lines in July 1943.

A similar modification applied to the wing. The so called 'universal' wing was first introduced on the P-47D-20-RE and this was designed to carry a variety of either long-range fuel tanks, bombs or rockets. Stronger shackles capable of lifting a 91 gallon long-range fuel tank were fitted under the fuselage, and with wing tanks fitted, the total range of the Thunderbolt was extended to 1,800 miles at an average speed of 195 mph at 10,000 feet. Paddle-blade airscrews of increased diameter were fitted to absorb the full power of the uprated engines and increased the climb to altitude rate by 400 feet a minute.

It was with this version of the P-47 that the USAAF did much of its escort work before the arrival of large quantities of P-51 Mustangs in the ETO. Thunderbolts escorted their 'big friends' to the target and on the return descended to low-level, using their

The eight .50 inch machine-guns in the wings of this Thunderbolt can be seen in this picture

powerful armament to hit opportunity targets on German airfields, roads and railways before returning to England.

The Farmingdale plant built 2,550 P-47Ds and the associated production line at Evansville built 3,743. In all 12,608 machines of this variety were produced, if the P-47Gs built by Curtiss-Wright at Buffalo are counted.

The Thunderbolt was also used by many foreign air forces during World War 2. The Soviet Union was given 203 P-47Ds under Lease-Lend, of which 196 reached their destination. A further 88 were supplied to Brazil and one Brazilian P-47D squadron operated with the 12th Air Force in Italy from November 11 1944. The Mexican Air Force had 25 examples and their 201st Fighter Squadron was due to serve with United States Forces in the South Pacific but it had not left Mexico by the time Japan was defeated.

The RAF used the P-47D in the Far East, having 240 machines on the Burmese Front. 16 RAF squadrons were equipped with the type, which was used for low-level bombing and strafing missions by the end of the war.

Of the remaining Allied Air Forces

the Free French, who had 446 P-47Ds, used the machine in the Middle East, Italy and in France itself after the landings in 1944. These aircraft continued in service with *l'Armée de l'Air* after the war in the French campaign against rebel units in Algeria.

The advent of the V-1 flying bombs necessitated a further development of the Thunderbolt which was hurriedly produced to meet the threat. Three P-47D airframes were fitted with the R-2800-57(C) and the larger CH-5 turbo supercharger which developed, under emergency power and with water injection, 2,800 hp at 32,500 feet. The aircraft were fitted with air brakes under the wings to slow the aircraft down after diving on its quarry. The prototypes were eventually designated YP-47Ms and subsequently 130 production aircraft were built. Most of these operated in France after D-Day against V-1 targets.

The P-47N Thunderbolt shown here was a version designed for the war in the Pacific in which its longer range was important. It also had square cut wing tips which made it immediately recognisable against the other versions of the aircraft.

The second prototype YP-47M was later fitted with a new wing with which it flew as the XP-47N in September 1944. This was, in fact, the final production version of the Thunderbolt and the only one intended expressly for operations in the Pacific theatre. Here long range was the principal requirement and the P-47N employed the longer fuselage of the later variants and a new strengthened wing of slightly greater span and area. The wings housed two 77.4 gallon fuel tanks and with external fuel a formidable 954 gallons could be carried. This gave the Thunderbolt its ultimate range of 2,350 miles.

A total of 1,667 of this last version of the Thunderbolt was produced and it reached squadrons in the Pacific area in 1945. The Thunderbolt flew escort missions with B-29s attacking the Japanese mainland from bases in Saipan and on many other long overwater trips. To gauge the extent of Thunderbolt operations in the Pacific during the first five months of 1945 the figures reveal that 1,677 sorties were flown during which 541 tons of bombs were dropped. In Europe Thunderbolts claimed the destruction of 86,000 railway wagons, 9,000 locomo-

Above *An interesting post-war Thunderbolt is this P-47D used as a drone target for air-to-air firing and early missile trials. Its attachment to Wright Field is obvious and a large size warning to any other aircraft being nosy (MAP).* **Below** *The second of three YP-47M Thunderbolts which used the Pratt and Whitney R-2800C engine and the Ch-5 turbo-supercharger of the XP-47J. This version, 150 of which were built, was designed to combat fast jet propelled aircraft of the Luftwaffe in Europe. The machine was eventually converted into the first XP-47N.*

The first of two XP-47H Thunderbolts which incorporated the 2,300 hp Chrysler XIV-2220-1 16-cylinder inverted-vee liquid cooled engine, designed for high altitude fighting.

American Fighters of World War 2

An unusual conversion of the Thunderbolt was the two-seat TP-47G. It was used for training purposes, though only two conversions from standard P-47D airframes were made.

tives, 6,000 armoured vehicles and tanks and 68,000 other vehicles by the end of the war. Thunderbolt pilots claimed 3,752 enemy aircraft in the air and a further 3,315 destroyed on the ground. It is estimated that a total of 1.35 million combat hours were flown and that the loss rate per sortie was less than seven per cent.

After the war the P-47D and N remained in service with USAAF units for ten years. They became the initial equipment of Tactical Air Command and Air Defence Command squadrons and eventually reached Air National Guard units in 1948. The final Thunderbolts passed out of operational service in 1955.

Known affectionately as the 'Jug', the Thunderbolt served in 58 fighter Groups of the USAAF at one time or another during World War 2. The 9th Air Force in Europe with a total of 16 Groups was the largest user and the total production was 15,660 machines.

In comparison with the Mustang not many Thunderbolts still remain in flying condition. There are, however, a number retained by museums, both in the United States and elsewhere. Several are still thought to be flying operationally with certain South American countries, though lack of spares and

the age of both airframes and engines must surely restrict the flying hours of the remaining aircraft.

Republic P-47D Thunderbolt Specification

Type Single-seat fighter and fighter bomber.

Power plant One 2,000 hp Pratt and Whitney R-2800-59 Double Wasp radial air-cooled engine.

Performance Max speed 429 mph at 30,000 feet. Range without external fuel 950 miles. Ceiling 40,000 feet.

Dimensions Span 40 feet 9 inches. Length 36 feet 2 inches. Height 14 feet 7 inches.

Armament Eight .50 inch machine-guns in the wings plus up to 2,500 lb bombs or ten rocket projectiles under wings.

Lockheed P-80 Shooting Star

Although not strictly coming within the category of this book, the P-80 Shooting Star has been included as it was America's first turbojet-driven fighter to enter operational service with the USAAF, although it did not do so in time to see action during World War 2.

The design was conceived in early 1943 as a direct takeover of the original work done by the Bell company after they had produced the Airacomet. Bell's extensive commitments in other directions led to the American authorities turning the project over to

Lockheed aircraft who retained the basic idea of building a fighter around the imported de Havilland H-1B Goblin jet engine to produce an extremely clean design on classical lines using the knowledge and techniques already acquired from piston-engined fighters then in service.

Redesignated XP-80, the prototype started to take shape in June 1943 and 143 days later the first aircraft was completed, flying for the first time on January 9 1944. During its initial trials it obtained a maximum speed of 502 mph at 20,480 feet and a service ceiling of 41,000 feet.

The prototype (44-83020) was built at the Lockheed plant at Burbank, California and was transferred to Edwards Air Force Base for its initial flight trials. It was an extremely sleek, low winged monoplane, having a laminar-flow wing cross section and the intakes for the jet faired into the fuselage immediately below a 'teardrop' canopy. Armament consisted of five .50 inch machine-guns grouped in the nose.

Production aircraft were equipped with the Allison-developed General Electric J33 engine rated at 3,750 lb st. This version also had an increased wing span and the fuselage length was 18 inches longer than on the prototype. A taller fin and rudder with a rounded top and a stronger undercarriage completed the modifications before 13 YP-80As were built for test purposes. The first of these was delivered in October 1944 and two aircraft

Photographic reconnaissance version of the F-80. Note the extra large long range fuel tanks on the wing tips. This aircraft named 'My Miss Carole B', was operated by the 155th PRS (Aviation Photo News).

reached Italy for operational trials shortly before VE Day.

Plans for large-scale production of the Shooting Star were laid in 1944, involving Lockheed as well as North American in the production contract. A total of 5,000 aircraft were due to be delivered but more than 3,000 of these were cancelled after VJ Day. Lockheed actually built 525 of the P-80A model and deliveries of these to the USAAF began in December 1945.

It was soon seen that to increase the range of the P-80 it was necessary to have external fuel, and wing tip long-range tanks were fitted and provision was made for underwing bombs or additional fuel tanks. An interesting feature of the early Shooting Stars was that an overall light grey finish was intended for use in sealing all skin joints. This, however, was found to be too difficult to maintain under field conditions and was eventually discarded in favour of a natural metal finish.

The Shooting Star came into its own during the Korean conflict in June 1950. Before this several world speed records were either attempted or gained by P-80s. A specially modified version for an attempt on the World Air

American Fighters of World War 2

An F-80 Shooting Star of the 8th Fighter Bomber Wing named 'Southern Comfort' seen during the Korean conflict. This aircraft was from the last production batch of the type.

Speed Record had a uprated J33-A-23 engine with water-alcohol injection, clipped wings, a smaller cockpit canopy and a high speed finish. On June 19 1947 this aircraft was flown by Colonel Albert Boyd and established a record of 623.8 mph.

Lockheed P-80 Shooting Star
Specification
Type Single-seat fighter.

Power plant One 3,850 lb st General Electric J33-GE-9 turbojet.

Performance Max speed 558 mph at 10,000 feet. Range 625 miles. Ceiling 45,000 feet.

Dimensions Span 38 feet 10½ inches. Length 34 feet 6 inches. Height 11 feet 4 inches.

Armament Six 0.5 inch machine-guns in the nose plus provision for two 500 or 1,000 lb bombs or drop tanks under the wings.

section two

US Navy and Marine Corps aircraft

Brewster F2A Buffalo

Up until 1936 the United States Navy had relied on successive highly manoeuvrable biplane fighters for fleet defence, but it was obvious that this type of aircraft was rapidly reaching its performance peak and to maintain air superiority it was necessary to use monoplane aircraft with retracting undercarriages.

Accordingly a contract was placed with the Brewster Aircraft Corporation on June 22 1936 for the start of design and construction of what was to become the first monoplane fighter equipping a US Navy squadron. The design bore a distinct family resemblance to the earlier biplanes in that it had a short stubby fuselage and a deep cockpit with plenty of room for the pilot. The wing was mid-mounted and of low aspect ratio. Its undercarriage retracted into the fuselage

and it was armed with two .50 inch machine-guns on the engine and later had two wing guns added after the style of its predecessors.

The new aircraft, designated XF2A-1, made its first flight in December 1937 and was delivered to the Navy a year later. Meanwhile, the first production contract had been placed for 54 of these aircraft, the first of which was rolled out in June 1939. They differed from the prototype in having a slightly less powerful engine and a larger fin and rudder.

The delivery of the first 11 F2A-1s was made in 1940 and ten of these went into service with VF-3 on board the USS *Saratoga*. The remaining 43 aircraft on the original contract did not reach the Navy and were sold to Finland early in 1940 as part of the urgently needed supplies to combat the Russian attack at that time.

Instead, the Navy were offered 40 F2A-2s as replacements and these were fitted with a 1,200 hp engine and the rudder was yet again redesigned. Other changes included an electric, rather than hydraulic, propeller and the addition of a high-altitude carburettor system. Testing of the prototype of this aircraft began in July 1939 and production deliveries started in September 1940.

The third and final order placed by the US Navy was for 108 F2A-3s in January 1941 which were delivered between July and December of that

One of 44 Brewster Buffalos purchased by Finland from the United States for use against the Russians during the Winter War in 1940 (Kalevi Keskinen).

American Fighters of World War 2

Cockpit interior of a Dutch Buffalo (via Tom Young).

year. Features of this model included increased armour protection for the pilot, self-sealing fuel tanks, improved equipment and consequently a greater all-up weight. This affected the aircraft's performance and the F2A was never greatly liked by Navy pilots.

The second squadron to be equipped with F2As was VF-2 on board USS *Lexington* and VS-201 used a small number on the escort carrier *Long Island*. One Marine squadron, VMF-221, also flew F2A-3s during the aircraft's operational life. As far as is known the fighter only took part in the sea battle at Midway when the Marine squadron already mentioned suffered major losses.

In the meantime the Brewster Aircraft Corporation had obtained several export orders for land-based versions of the fighter. The Belgian Air Force ordered 40 machines under the designation B-339 and the British Purchasing Commission ordered a further 170 which were immediately named 'Buffalo'.

Unfortunately, deliveries of the Belgian order could not be completed before that country was invaded. One, possibly two, aircraft in crates reached the French port of Bordeaux in June 1940 and were subsequently captured by the Germans. Others were being ferried to Europe on board the French aircraft carrier *Berne* at the time of the

French collapse and the ship was diverted to Martinique where the Buffaloes were disembarked. Here they remained and as far as is known were not used before being relegated to scrap.

The remainder of the Belgian contract was taken over by the Fleet Air Arm and six aircraft were taken on strength by No 805 Squadron and operated alongside Fulmars from March 1941. These machines were despatched to Crete to provide fighter cover for the Naval base at Suda Bay but proved totally inadequate against modern German fighters.

Trials were undertaken by No 71 Squadron in the RAF but the Buffalo was rejected as a first-line fighter. However, Nos 21 and 453 Squadrons of the RAAF, Nos 67 and 243 Squadrons of the RAF and No 488 Squadron of the RNZAF were equipped with the Buffalo in Malaya for the defence of Singapore.

The addition of armour, heavier armament and extra operational equipment severely restricted the manoeuvrability of these aircraft and the climb rate and ceiling were greatly reduced. It was therefore no match for the Japanese Zero fighters which opposed it when the Japanese invaded. Although the squadrons involved put up a valiant defence they were shot out of the sky by the superior Japanese aircraft and the remnants retired to join the American Volunteer Group in the aerial defence of Burma.

In an attempt to bolster their Far East air forces the Dutch ordered 72 of the Brewster fighters in 1940 followed by another order for 20 fitted with a more powerful engine. The Dutch had taken delivery of 30 B-339D fighters, as they were called, by early December 1941, and a squadron was despatched to Malaya where it saw action against the Japanese. The remnants of this unit were withdrawn to Sumatra and they fought continuously against the Japanese advance through the East Indies. A further 20 aircraft that had been held in reserve joined those that escaped from Malaya and, fitted with bombs, actually sank a Japanese destroyer and damaged a number of cargo-carrying ships during the invasion.

In all the F2A had an undistinguished career but at least it should be remembered as being the first of a long line of US Navy monoplane fighters all having the same configuration of radial engine, short stubby fuselage and midwing construction. A total of 507 F2As were built before production was terminated in March 1942.

Brewster F2A (Buffalo) Specification
Type Single-seat fleet fighter and fighter-bomber.
Power plant One 1,200 hp Wright R-1820-40 9-cylinder radial, air-cooled engine.
Performance Max speed 321 mph at 16,500 feet. Cruising speed 258 mph. Range 965 miles. Ceiling 33,200 feet.
Dimensions Span 35 feet. Length 26 feet 4 inches. Height 12 feet 1 inch.
Armament Four .50 inch Browning machine-guns and racks for two 100 lb bombs.

Grumman F4F Wildcat

The US Navy, having for so long depended on biplanes, thought it prudent to insure against the failure of their first choice, the Brewster F2A, by ordering another monoplane at the same time. The Grumman Aircraft Corporation had for long been producing Navy aircraft and were thus the logical choice to produce the standby machine.

An order was therefore placed on March 2 1936 for the XF4F-1, which, although it started life as a biplane, was very shortly converted to monoplane configuration. The order was confirmed by the US Navy on July 28 1936 as the XF4F-2. As it happened, the Grumman design was to survive throughout the war in various forms and the Brewster machine only saw limited action.

Although the XF4F-2 had a singularly inauspicious start its shape followed the characteristic rotund fuselage design, like its Brewster contemporary, and under the manufacturer's designation G-36 flew for the first time on September 2 1937. It was delivered to the US Navy test centre at Anacostia on December 23. Power was supplied by a Pratt & Whitney R-1830-66 Twin Wasp radial engine producing 1,050 hp for take-off and 900 hp at 10,000 feet. Its performance was somewhat disappointing and although slightly faster than the Brewster F2A was inferior in many other respects.

Having accepted the Brewster design, US Navy interest in the F4F waned, and the aircraft was returned to Grumman who decided to carry out a major rework on the aircraft which involved several radical changes.

In the first instance the engine was changed to a unit having a two-stage

The first prototype of the Wildcat, apart from having mid-wings, differed almost entirely in outline shape from the production aircraft. Known as the XF4F-2, it first appeared in 1937.

American Fighters of World War 2

supercharger which gave 1,200 hp for take-off and 2,000 hp at 19,000 feet. The airframe was similarly altered and included a new set of wings with span increased by four feet, a redesigned tail unit, altered armament configuration and the addition of an airscrew spinner.

The revised prototype resumed trials on February 12 1939 and after further minor modifications was extremely successful.

Grumman's faith in the new design was upheld when, during Navy trials, the aircraft attained a speed of 335.5 mph and recorded a height of 21,300 feet. The potential of the aircraft was now clearly established and the US Navy ordered 54 aircraft, the first of which was ready for flight in February 1940.

In the same way that Brewster did with their machine, Grumman offered the F4F for export and succeeded in obtaining orders from the French Government for 81 and the Greek Navy for 30.

Like many other French orders placed in America, none could be delivered before the French capitulation, and the British Purchasing Commission in Washington took over the entire batch. The first five were delivered to Canada and the remainder reached the United Kingdom in

The first production Wildcat was the F4F-3A, seen here shortly after rollout. Note the window in the fuselage under the wing to allow the pilot a downward view.

October 1940 where they entered service with No 804 Squadron of the Fleet Air Arm. It is also significant that one of these machines, now named Martlet I, became the first US aircraft in British service to shoot down a German aircraft in World War 2. This occurred on December 25 1940 when two Martlets patrolling over Scapa Flow intercepted and shot down a Junkers Ju 88 reconnaissance aircraft.

The Royal Navy accepted the Martlet with open arms as it proved to be equal or superior to anything they had in service at that time. In fact the Martlet entered service with the Fleet Air Arm before deliveries began to the US Navy. The British used the aircraft under operational conditions and after America entered the war passed on all the valuable information they had gained about the machine. By December 1940 22 F4Fs had been delivered to the US Navy and initial deliveries went to VF-4 (USS *Ranger*) and VF-7 (USS *Wasp*). In 1941 VF-42 and VF-71 were equipped as well as US Marine squadrons VMF-121, 211 and 221. Grumman received further US Navy orders for 95 additional F4Fs which went to VF-6 and Marine unit VMF-111.

By the end of 1941 the Navy and Marine Corps had together 183 F4F-3s and 65 F4F-3As, mostly in the United States or on board the *Ranger* and *Wasp*. However, two Marine squadrons were based in Hawaii when the Japanese surprise attack on Pearl Harbour was launched and nine aircraft were destroyed on the ground.

Above *The Wildcat bore the brunt of the first aerial combat between the Japanese and American carrier fleets. These aircraft, all F4F-4s, were photographed during the Battle of Midway.* **Below** *Grumman production line in 1941. At least 11 Wildcats can be seen in various stages of manufacture together with two Grumman Goose amphibians for the Royal Navy.*

Later that day the same squadron, VMF-211, lost seven more aircraft on the ground at Wake Island when the secondary Japanese task force attacked. The remaining Marine aircraft scored several victories over Japanese bombers before they too were shot down by the vastly superior Japanese forces.

Meanwhile, in the Fleet Air Arm the Martlet II had been delivered. A total of 100 aircraft were ordered and included many of those originally destined for Greece. The latter were designated Mk III and, like the II, had folding wings. These versions were the first to see carrier-borne service with the Royal Navy and operated from the small escort carriers then coming into service on the North Atlantic convoy routes protecting shipping against attacks from German Fw 200 Condors. No 802 Squadron's Martlets destroyed no less than four of these Luftwaffe machines in the last months of 1941.

By now the American aircraft industry had produced sufficient F4Fs to

American Fighters of World War 2

An excellent picture of the Grumman F4F-4 Wildcat.

equip all US carrier fighter squadrons and the type, now named Wildcat, was the sole American shipboard fighter in service for the first half of the war, taking part in all major battles and destroying 905 enemy aircraft between 1941 and 1943 for the loss of only 178 machines.

So great was the demand for the Wildcat that on April 18 1942 Eastern Aircraft was made a second production source with a contract for 1,800 machines. Eastern had a group of five factories previously assembling General Motors cars and the Wildcat's designation was changed to FM-1 for the aircraft built at this source. The first production Wildcat flew on August 31 1942 and some 840 were delivered in the first 12 months plus about 300 going to Britain as Martlet Vs.

The British aircraft took part in many well known operations apart from continuing on escort carriers in the North Atlantic and on the route to Russia round the North Cape. The invasion of North Africa by Allied forces and the landings on Madagascar which involved Nos 881 and 882 Squadrons operating from HMS *Illustrious* were part of these.

The advent of the small CVE, or escort carrier as it was known, led to the development of the final Wildcat version, the FM-2. This combined a more powerful Wright Cyclone engine with a lighter airframe to obtain better take-off performance from the short carrier decks. Grumman built two prototypes, designated XF4F-8s, which flew from the company factory at Bethpage on November 8 1942, and production contracts were let for 1,265 examples. This version had a taller fin and rudder and a water injection system for the engine. A total of 114

escort carriers saw service on the Allied side before the end of the war. Almost all of these were equipped with Martlet or Wildcat fighters and they fought with great distinction in all of the major sea battles, in convoy operations, the Pacific invasion forces and those that landed in Europe in 1944.

Grumman F4F Wildcat Specification
Type Single-seat shipboard fighter.
Power plant One 1,200 hp Pratt & Whitney R-1830-76 Twin Wasp radial air-cooled engine.
Performance Max speed 328 mph at 21,000 feet. Range 845 miles on internal fuel. Ceiling 37,500 feet.
Dimensions Span 38 feet. Length 28 feet 9 inches. Height 9 feet 2½ inches.
Armament Four or six .50 inch machine-guns and two 100 lb bombs.

Grumman F6F Hellcat

The move of Wildcat production from the main Grumman factories to those of General Motors proved provident as Grumman's next fighter, the F6F Hellcat, took most of the parent factory's production capacity from 1942 onwards.

The US Navy urgently needed a follow-on aircraft for the Wildcat and Grumman's design staff, having assessed the need shown up by early battles against Japanese Zeros, produced a much more powerful fighter based around the Pratt & Whitney R-2800 Double Wasp engine. The aircraft that first flew on July 30 1944 was the harbinger of what was to become one of the most significant fighters in the US Navy's armoury during World War 2. Being the second generation of the mid-wing stubby fuselaged monoplane fighters that the US Navy had accepted, it incorporated the power and armament that was perhaps lacking in its predecessor the Wildcat. So successful was this design that it was used in many roles during its service career including those of night fighter and ground-attack aircraft.

Production and development of the Hellcat was rapid and the first squadron to receive them was VF-9 on January 16 1943 on board the USS *Essex*. They were used in combat for the first time operated by VF-5 from the USS *Yorktown* during an attack on Marcus Island on August 31 1943, a mere 18 months after the prototype's first flight.

The Hellcat rapidly replaced the Wildcat on board the main fleet carriers and was destined to remain a standard fighter aircraft of the US Navy for the remainder of the war. It also saw service during Korean operations in the 1950s.

Britain's Fleet Air Arm also took the Hellcat under a Lease-Lend arrangement. The first aircraft joined the Fleet Air Arm in July 1943 with No 800 Squadron and took part, on board the light escort carrier *Emperor*, in anti-shipping strikes off the Norwegian coast in December. The Hellcat's main service with the Royal Navy, however, was in the Far East. With the lessening of tension on North Atlantic convoys and the adequate use of the Martlet still in service, it was found that the heavier fleet carriers could be released for service in the Far East and with their fighter squadrons equipped with the Hellcat they took part in most

Left *The F6F Hellcat was a worthy successor to the Wildcat. This machine belongs to VF20 squadron.* **Below** *F6F Hellcat of Photo Training Squadron VD2 being flown by Lt Jg Eddie Bowmar.*

of the operations in the south west Pacific area. A total of 930 Hellcats were supplied to the Fleet Air Arm and a further 80 radar-equipped equivalents entered service with Nos 891 and 892 Squadrons as NFIIs. Ten other FAA Squadrons operated the Hellcat up to VJ Day when most were returned to America at the end of the Leasing agreement.

During its service life, the Hellcat differed very little in basic outline shape. The only major sub-version was the F6F-5 which had a slightly modified cowling and cockpit canopy. This version also had provision for 2,000 lb of bombs under the centre section and strongpoints for six rockets under the outer wings. Armament of 20 mm cannon usually replaced the inner of the six .50 inch machine-guns in the wings on this model and a number were converted for night fighter duties. These were designated F6F-5N and had a radar bulge on the starboard wing. They were destined to

High over the US Pacific coastline a squadron of Hellcats under training. These aircraft show the mid-war two-tone blue and white colour scheme used by the US Navy at that time.

remain in service with the US Navy and its reserve units until long after the end of World War 2.

Official figures show that US Navy carrier-based Hellcats were credited with the destruction of 4,947 enemy aircraft in air-to-air combat, with another 209 claimed by land-based Navy and Marine Units during World War 2. This accounted for almost 75 per cent of all the Navy's air-to-air victories. Production of the Hellcat ended in November 1945 with a total of 12,275 built.

Grumman F6F Hellcat Specification

Type Single-seat shipboard fighter and fighter-bomber.
Power plant One 2,000 hp Pratt & Whitney R-2800-10 radial engine.
Performance Max speed 335 mph at sea level. Range 1,090 miles with 125 gall drop tanks. Ceiling 38,400 feet.
Dimensions Span 42 feet 10 inches. Length 33 feet 7 inches. Height 13 feet 1 inch.
Armament Six .50 inch machine-guns in the wings, 2,000 lb bombs or six 5-inch rockets.

Grumman F7F Tigercat

The development of Naval aircraft by the Grumman company during World War 2 was little short of miraculous. Having started the war with outdated, ill-equipped aircraft, the US Navy had in the space of five years the most powerful carrier-borne air force in the world; it had established itself as the supreme sea power and has continued with this policy to the present day. Much of this development centred around four aircraft designed and produced by the Grumman company during that time.

Having produced two highly efficient shipborne fighters in the Wildcat and Hellcat, Grumman were asked to develop the US Navy's first tricycle undercarriage, twin-engined fighter in the early stages of the war, and apart from being unique in that it was the largest fighter of its type, the new machine, known as the F7F Tigercat, was also one of the first aircraft to be

designed specifically for operation from a new class of aircraft carrier. These ships were the 45,000 ton USS *Midway* class, several of which have continued in service until recent years.

The Tigercat stemmed from a prototype twin-engine fighter which was proposed as early as June 1938 known as the XF5F-1. This machine suffered a number of shortcomings but it provided a useful basis for the development of a larger twin-engine fighter ordered from Grumman on June 30 1941. This aircraft, given the Grumman type No G-51, became the US Navy's first twin-engined aircraft to enter quantity production and although classified as a fighter was designed to operate in the tactical support role as well.

The Tigercat was a shoulder wing all-metal aircraft powered by two 2,100 hp R-2800-22W Double Wasp engines and had an extremely heavy armament of four 20 mm cannon with 200 rounds per gun in the wing roots and four .50 inch machine-guns in the nose. It was also designed to carry the standard US torpedo beneath the fuselage and provision was made for two 1,000 lb bombs under the wings.

The first of two XF7F-1s flew in December 1943, by which time the pressing needs of the amphibious forces, then engaged in operations designed to recapture the string of islands across the Pacific previously taken so rapidly by the advancing Japanese, led to an order for 500 of the new Tigercats almost straight from the drawing board.

Grumman's twin-engined Navy fighter, the F7F-3N Tigercat. This version was a post-war example designed as a ship-board night fighter. It saw active service during the Korean war (Aviation Photo News).

Deliveries of the first F7Fs started in April 1944 but operational problems and changing requirements led to restrictions in the production programme and delays in the issue of the aircraft to operational squadrons. After the first 33 examples had been delivered the 35th machine was completed as a two-seat variant designated F7F-2N. This was the first night fighter version and Grumman built 65 of them, including the prototype. Production then started on a further 189 F7F-3s which were similar to the original single-seat model but had different engines.

The Tigercat came too late to see operational service with either the US Navy or Marine Corps squadrons and all post VJ-Day orders were cancelled, the total production not exceeding 189 machines.

The Tigercat was an attractive aircraft visually but its operational service with the US Navy was marred by the fact that development of jet aircraft in both the fighter and fighter-bomber roles overtook its usefulness, and although its production was a milestone in the history of United States Naval aircraft it did not see sufficient service to justify its excellent qualities.

Grumman F7F-2 Tigercat
Specification
Type   Single-seat shipboard day and night fighter.
Power plant   Two 2,100 hp Pratt & Whitney R-2800-22W radial engines.
Petformance   Max speed 363 mph at sea level. Range 960 miles. Ceiling 39,800 feet.
Dimensions   Span 51 feet 6 inches. Length 45 feet 4½ inches. Height 16 feet 7 inches.
Armament   Four 20 mm cannon and four .50 inch machine-guns.

Grumman F8F-1 Bearcat

The F8F Bearcat was the last of four US Navy fighters produced by Grumman during the war. It was also the last operational machine to be named as part of the 'cat' series before the advent of the F-14 Tomcat which has recently entered service with the US Navy. The Bearcat was not ordered until November 1943 and at that time the specification called for a low altitude fighter with superior climb and manoeuvrability performance to overcome the type of attack then being made on US Navy Fleets in the Pacific area.

It was a much smaller machine than the preceding Wildcat or Hellcat types but was rushed into service with the same rapidity as his predecessors. The first prototype Bearcat flew on August 21 1944 within ten months of the development contract being placed and production deliveries started a mere five months later.

The Bearcat retained the distinctive short stubby outline similar to the other Grumman single-seater fighters, and it was in fact the design team's considered opinion that nothing smaller could be built to take both the powerful Double Wasp engine, specified fuel load, armament and armour protection. An unusual design feature which was eventually abandoned was the provision of a breakpoint at the wing tips where explosive bolts operated automatically if the aircraft was handled too violently in flight. The tips were designed to fail at selected points should the wings be overstressed in flight so that a symmetric situation could be maintained and the aircraft, plus pilot, brought back to base.

Two prototypes of the new Grumman design were ordered by the Navy and the performance of these was confirmed in flight as being one of the fastest aircraft then in existence. The aircraft had a top speed of 424 mph and an initial rate of climb of 4,800 feet-minute which outclassed any other contemporary aircraft. For a

The last of the Grumman line of piston-engined Navy fighters was the F8F Bearcat. This version is a F8F-1B armed with four 20 mm cannon. 100 aircraft of this variant were built.

period the Bearcat held the world record for the fastest climb to 10,000 feet. Armament comprised four .50 inch guns in the wings and bomb racks for two 1,000 lb bombs or two drop tanks. Contracts for the production of 2,023 F8F-1s were placed with Grumman on October 6 1944, and as the Wildcat production at General Motors was being phased out, these were to be supplemented by a further contract on February 5 1945 for 1,876 Bearcats to be designated F3M-1.

Deliveries began in February 1945 and the first operational squadron, VF-19, received its initial equipment on May 21 1945. The war ended whilst this squadron was working up and brought with it the cancellation of the General Motors programme and a considerable cut in the Grumman contract to a mere 765 aircraft. Other US Navy squadrons continued to re-equip with the Bearcat during 1946 and 1947 and in all a total of 24 squadrons received the type by 1948. In addition to the original order after reductions Grumman received a further contract for 100 F8F-1Bs with 20 mm cannon replacing the machine-guns in the wings. Another contract called for 36 F8F-1Ns equipped as night fighters.

As it was obvious that the Bearcat was going to continue in US Navy service for some time after the war and until jet-powered equipment was available in sufficient numbers to replace piston engine aircraft, Grum-

man put forward a general improvement programme producing the F8F-2 in 1948. This had the 20 mm cannon armament, a revised engine cowling, taller fin and rudder and other minor changes. The company built 293 of these aircraft plus 12 night fighter versions and 60 photographic reconnaissance aircraft designated F8F-2P. The production of the Bearcat finally ended in May 1949, at which time 12 US Navy squadrons were equipped with the later version. Another 12 were still flying the F8F-1 but by mid-1949 the Navy began to withdraw its Bearcats from front line units, passing many on to reserve squadrons before the last F8F-2Ps were taken off strength in late 1952. Subsequently Bearcats were modified as drone control aircraft and a large number were sold to the French for operations in Indo-China and also to the Royal Thai Air Force.

Grumman F8F-1 Bearcat Specification

Type Single-seat shipboard interceptor fighter and fighter-bomber.

Power plant One 2,100 hp Pratt & Whitney R-2800-34W radial air-cooled engine.

Performance Max speed 382 mph at sea level. Range 1,105 miles. Ceiling 38,700 feet.

The F8F-2P was a photo reconnaissance version of the Bearcat. This one is serialled 121546 and also illustrates the fuselage-mounted long range fuel tank.

Dimensions Span 35 feet 10 inches. Length 28 feet 3 inches. Height 13 feet 10 inches.

Armament Four .50 inch machine-guns plus two 1,000 lb bombs or four 5-inch rockets.

Vought F4U Corsair

The Vought Corsair ranks equally in the US Navy with the Mustang and Thunderbolt in the Army Air Force. It was in production longer than any other US fighter in World War 2 and has many other claims to fame. Apart from being credited with an 11 to one ratio of kills to losses in action against Japanese aircraft, it was also the last piston-engine fighter in production for any of the US services. Not only did it operate from United States Navy carriers but in many cases was a land-based operational aircraft for both fighter and fighter-bomber operations.

It is also interesting to note that the Corsair first originated as far back as 1938 when it was entered for a single-seat shipboard fighter competition issued by the US Navy, and a proto-type was ordered from what was then the Chance Vought Aircraft company as the XF4U-1 on June 30 1938. Given the Vought type number of V-166B, the design team led by 'Tex' Beisel produced an attractive looking machine around the new and yet untried R-2800 Double Wasp engine and featuring an inverted gull wing configuration. This was selected in

Post-war Corsair : a French Navy F4U-7 serialled 133699. These machines were used in Indo-China, before the French withdrew, and later in Algeria.

The XF4U-1 Corsair prototype which became the first US fighter of any type to exceed .400 mph in level flight. It was flown for the first time on May 29 1940.

F4U-2 Corsairs of a US Navy squadron on board the CVE Windham Bay in 1944 line up for take off.

Post-war Corsair : a factory fresh AU-1 Bu No 133843 in the overall Gloss Sea Blue colour scheme typical of the 1950s period.

order to provide the necessary ground clearance for the very large Hamilton Standard propeller whilst keeping the undercarriage length and ground angle to a minimum. At that time the Double Wasp engine was providing 8,850 hp and the Corsair was given an armament of both .30 inch and .50 inch machine-guns in the engine cowling and wings. Provision for ten light bombs was made under the wings and the intention was that these should be dropped on enemy bomber formations in an unconventional method of attack.

The F4U-1D was adapted to carry either a long range fuel tank or bombs. This machine is seen with a 1,000 lb bomb under the centre section.

The XF4U-1 flew for the first time on May 29 1940 and its sensational performance was immediately apparent. Before the end of the year the prototype had flown at 404 mph, faster than any other US fighter in the air. The US Navy accordingly ordered production of 584 Corsairs and delivery of the first aircraft from the production line started on October 3 1942, four months after the first flight of a prototype machine. The first aircraft went to VF-12 and had several armament modifications. Self-sealing fuel tanks and armour protection was added and the cockpit was located three feet further aft to allow for additional fuel to be carried in the fuselage. The moving of the cockpit position adversely affected the pilot's view

An experimental version of the Corsair, the F4U-1C was fitted with four 20 mm cannons.

and carrier landing trials on board the USS *Sangamon* in September 1942 led to doubts being raised as to the suitability of the Corsair for carrier operations. Consequently, the first F4U-1s were issued to land-based Marine units starting with VMF-124. The aircraft first saw combat on February 13 1943 at Bougainville and within the next month the first Navy squadron, VF-12, also land-based, began operations from New Georgia.

The Corsair did not become deck qualified until April 1943. In addition to the problems of poor visibility from the cockpit, other difficulties such as the aircraft's tendency to swing badly on touchdown, and bounce badly because of its stiff landing gear, were noted.

To overcome the deficiencies of the Corsair as a deck-landing aircraft, a frameless clear-view type canopy was introduced and the cockpit itself raised by seven inches to improve forward vision. This version, known as the F4U-1A, also had its directional stability improved by increasing the

Above *US Marine Corps Corsairs showing the unusual application of the Marines badge on the nose cowling.* **Below** *Corsair fighter bombers each carrying two 1,000 lb bombs taxi for take off from a Pacific island base.*

American Fighters of World War 2

height of the tail wheel leg. By adding a solid instead of a pneumatic type tyre and adding a small spoiler on the starboard wing leading edge, it was found that the Corsair's performance came within safety standards for deck landing. These changes were made on the 689th production aircraft and following successful trials performed by VF-301 on board the USS *Gambier Bay* in April 1944, the fighter was finally cleared for use aboard US Navy carriers.

To speed production, contracts were placed with the Brewster and Goodyear companies for versions of the basic Corsair design. These were designated F3A-1 and FG-1 respectively and both incorporated the raised cockpit hood already mentioned. Some Corsairs were fitted with four 20 mm cannon in the wings in place of the machine-guns under the designation F4U-1C, whilst others were used as fighter-bombers, having fittings for a long range tank under the fuselage and two 1,000 lb bombs or eight 5-inch rockets under the wings.

Above *F4U-1Ds in late 1943 on the island of Iwo Jima accompanied by a Privateer, two Mustangs and a B-29 Superfortress.* **Below** *The F4U-1A belonging to US Navy ace Lt Ira Kepford when serving with VF-17 in the New Georgia area in February 1944.*

US Navy and Marine Corps aircraft

The Corsair entered service with the Royal Navy in 1944 and on April 3 of that year Corsair IIs of No 1834 Squadron from HMS *Victorious* took part and operated as fighter escort for the attacks on the German battleship *Tirpitz*. In all 2,012 Corsairs were supplied to the Royal Navy under Lease-Lend whilst another 370 went to the Royal New Zealand Air Force. The latter were used in the south west Pacific area and operated by three squadrons.

The Fleet Air Arm Corsairs were slightly modified for British service. They needed some 16 inches clipped off the wing tips to permit stowage below decks on British carriers. British aircraft also became fitted with a bulged front canopy to improve the forward view and allowed the pilot to raise his seat. Rocket rails were fitted under the wings and the earlier machines were rapidly given provision for a ventral drop tank beneath the fuselage to increase the range. A total of 19 Fleet Air Arm squadrons were equipped with the Corsair during the war.

On January 6 1942 Vought submitted a proposal for the F4U-2 radar-equipped night fighter and the mock-up was ready for inspection by the US Navy on January 28. Pressure of normal production led to the cancellation of an initial order for 50 so 12 standard F4U-1s were converted at Quonset Point, Rhode Island, and six machines were given to VF(N)-75 which went into action from Munda Strip on New Georgia. Later, VF(N)-101 operated in turn from USS *Essex, Hornet* and *Intrepid.* Another in-service modification was the F4U-1P, which had cameras fitted for reconnaissance duties.

The use of a turbo-supercharged version of the Double Wasp engine was projected as early as 1941 and in March 1942 Vought received a contract for three prototypes to test this engine. Work proceeded on low priority throughout the war and the first XF4U-3 did not appear until 1946 with an R-2800-16 power unit. A number of FG-3s, which were the Goodyear production line equivalent, were ordered, but only 13 were completed. The next major production version of the Corsair was therefore the F4U-4 which first flew on April 19 1944 with a 2,100 hp Double Wasp engine. The additional power from this engine increased the speed of the Corsair to 446 mph and other small changes, including a further redesign of the cockpit, a revised canopy and a new armour-plated bucket seat were incorporated. The standard six .50 inch machine-gun armament was retained and the carburettor intake

The F4U-4 was the final wartime production model of the Corsair. It featured a raised cockpit canopy and a revised air intake from the wing roots to the engine cowling. This machine belongs to VMF-214.

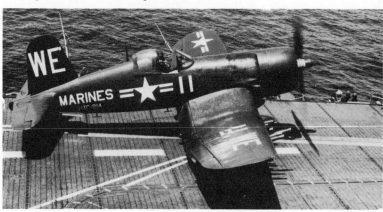

he Corsair was still in production
fter the war and this version, a F4U-7
vas one of the type exported to the
rench Aeronavale. It also saw service
n the Korean war.

arrying eight 5 inch HVAR rockets,
his F4U-4B Corsair packed a powerful
unch.

duct was moved from the wing leading
edges to beneath the engine cowling.
Various production variants of the
basic -4 aircraft included cannon
armament, a night fighter version and
some camera-equipped aircraft.
Goodyear built 200 as the FG-4 whilst
Vought production of these variants
totalled 2,356.

In spite of large scale cancellation of
contracts following VJ Day, production of the F4U-4 by Vought continued

until 1947. Goodyear production was stopped and the Goodyear-developed low-altitude versions, the F2G-1 and the F2G-2 with folding wings, were cancelled after five of each had been completed.

In 1946 Vought produced a new Corsair variant, the XF4U-5, by fitting a 2,300 hp two stage R-2800-32W engine and four 20 mm wing guns to an earlier -4 variant. To meet immediate requirements for a carrier-based fighter bomber and night fighter the Navy purchased 223 of these aircraft and a further 315 night fighters. A photographic version was also produced and 30 were acquired between 1947 and 1948. Yet another version, the XF4U-6, with additional armour protection, increased underwing load ability and other modifications to suit it for low altitude operation, was designed. This was redesignated AU-1 and went into production for use by US Marine squadrons operating in Korea. A total of 110 were built.

The last Corsair version, of which 90 were produced, was similar to the AU-1 but had yet another variant of the successful R-2800 engine. It was sup-plied to the US Navy and through th Military Aid Procurement programme to the French Aeronavale for use i Indo-China.

After the war Corsair production was transferred to Dallas as Chance Vought became part of United Aircraft Production ended in December 1952 after the aircraft had been on the line for more than ten years.

By VJ-Day United States Navy and Marines Corsairs in the Pacific theatre had destroyed no less than 2,140 enemy aircraft in air-to-air combat fo the loss of 189 of their own machines Operational sorties from February 1 1942 totalled 64,051, 54,470 of these being made from land bases while 9,581 were flown from carriers.

There were no less than seven US aces who flew the Corsair. All of these scored more than 18 kills and included Colonel Gregory M. 'Pappy' Boying

Post-war night fighter. One of the las versions of the Corsair was the F4U 5N equipped with four 20 mm canno and wing mounted radar. Underwing hard points for rockets or bombs wer still maintained.

Another view of the F4U-1A belonging to US Navy ace Lt Ira Kepford when serving with VF-17 in the New Georgia area in February 1944.

on, the CO of VMF-124, who had 28 enemy aircraft destroyed to his credit. He was closely followed by Major Joseph Foss who commanded VMF-122 and had 26 kills, whilst Lieutenant Robert M. Hanson with 25 victories scored 20 of these within 17 days.

The Corsair was the spearhead of the US Marine and US Navy fighter-bomber squadrons which flew 45 per cent of the combat sorties during the Korean War. Lieutenant Guy Bordelon, flying a F4U-5NL night fighter Corsair over Korea, shot down five North Korean aircraft to become the first Navy Corsair ace of the Korean War.

During the Pacific campaign the Japanese called the Corsair 'the whistling death', an apt name for such a versatile fighter. Perhaps the only other comment that can be added is that of Major George Axtell, who commanded VMF-411 and is quoted as saying that the Corsair was 'the best fighter there is. It's rugged. It's a workhorse. You can use it for anything including dive bombing and it is effective. You could shoot anything off or out of that plane and it still goes on'; with no fewer than 12,571 Corsairs built over the decade, there is no doubt that it was one of the finest US fighters ever built.

Vought F4U-1D Corsair Specification
Type Single-seat shipboard fighter and fighter-bomber.
Power plant One 2,250 hp Pratt & Whitney R-2800-8W Double Wasp radial air-cooled engine.
Performance Max speed 328 mph at sea level. Range 1,015 miles. Ceiling 37,000 feet.
Dimensions Span 40 feet 11 inches. Length 33 feet 4 inches. Height 15 feet 1 inch.
Armament Six .50 inch machine-guns in the wings. Two 1,000 lb bombs or eight 5-inch rockets.

Bibliography

United States Military Aircraft since 1908, by Gordon Swanborough and Peter M. Bowers. Putnam.

United States Navy Aircraft since 1911, by Gordon Swanborough and Peter M. Bowers. Putnam.

Warplanes of the Second World War, Fighters Vol 4, by William Green. Macdonald.

Lockheed P-38 Lightning, by Edward T. Maloney. Aero Publishers Inc.

Chance Vought F4U Corsair, by Edward T. Maloney and Uwe Feist. Aero Publishers Inc.

Republic P-47 Thunderbolt. Aero Publishers Inc.

Mustang at war, by Roger A. Freeman. Ian Allan Ltd.

North American P-51 Mustang, by Richard Ward. Osprey Publications Ltd.

Republic P-47 Thunderbolt, by Richard Ward. Osprey Publications Ltd.

Curtiss P-40D-N Warhawk, by Christopher F. Shores. Osprey Publications Ltd.

Classic Aircraft No 3, P-51 Mustang, by Roy Cross, Gerald Scarborough and Bruce Robertson. Patrick Stephens Ltd.

Profile Publications Nos 7, 8, 35, 47, 53, 80, 100, 106, 107, 136, 150, 165 and 217.

Magazines — *Aeroplane Spotter, Air Pictorial, Airfix Magazine, RAF Flying Review, Air International, Aeroplane Monthly, Aircraft Illustrated, Aviation News.*